adam
without
eden

HOPE FAR FROM HOME

SAMUEL C. WALKER

Adam Without Eden
Copyright © Samuel C. Walker 2015. All rights reserved.

Published by Stonebridge Publications.
StonebridgePublications.com

All scriptures marked KJV are taken from the King James Version of the Bible.
All scriptures marked JB are taken from the Jerusalem Bible used by permission. Darton, Longman & Todd - London, 1966.
All scriptures marked NJB are taken from the New Jerusalem Bible used by permission. Doubleday NY, NY 1985 - ISBN 0-385-14264-1.

Cover Photo: Samuel C. Walker
Author Photo: Aregawi Gebreigziabher.
Cover Design: Rob Trahan.
Copy Symbol: Colin D. Walker, after motif of St. Georges rock-hewn church, Lalibela, Ethiopia.

ISBN 13:978-1-940473-49-9
ISBN 13:978-940473-50-5 Ebook

Printed in the United States of America – all rights reserved.

Dedication

To my beautiful wife, Diane, mother to our children –
Chris, Hilary, Byron, Colin and Letebrhan

Confidant, muse, translator of my mind,
My African-Arabian Queen.
Many times have you gotten in my boat
Embarking to distant, pagan shores.
Together, navigating by faith and the stars,
We strode all earth's hemispheres,
Gleaning memories of God's faithfulness,
On our own Jesus-field trips.

And to my parents, Dale and Carla Walker, who taught me
a love of Scripture and a life quest for a bigger God.

Contents

Foreword

A man did not know his wife when he began to come back to life after a terrible injury. He knew she was his wife, but he had lost his understanding of his attraction to her and their intimate relationship. This type of loss is not unusual after major physical trauma.

When I began to emerge from the cloudy world of my severe spinal cord injury, in unimaginable, agonizing pain, I had lost a great deal of my understanding of my relationship to Jesus. I knew He was my savior. Yes, I knew He was God, that He willingly died to pay for my sin. But I was like the man who knew his wife to be his wife but couldn't recall the irresistible, yearning desire he must have once had to be intimate with her.

I have yearned for that intimate renewal of the relationship I must have once had with Jesus. So, I began to carefully quiz Christ-Following friends about who Jesus was to them. Shockingly, most of them cohabitate with Jesus, but they sleep in twin beds and their desire is friendly but not passionate. Could that have been me?

Reading "Adam Without Eden", painfully struggling to turn each page with my crippled, unfeeling fingers, I have begun to see that I maybe never knew the radical Jesus in the irresistible and intimate way I yearn for.

Do not read this book if you are satisfied with cohabitating with Jesus. But if you want to see the Jesus who chose slow-to-learn disciples like us, if you yearn to be a passionate newlywed, then I heartily recommend that you start to read this book. Then digest and read on. Examine who Sam reveals Jesus to be against what our Bible reveals. Go slowly. Most romances spring to life with surprising speed but grow deeply passionate over time and through trials.

Steve with Ginny Saint

Acknowledgment

No book is an island, or an original thought. Many folks have worked with me to produce *Adam Without Eden*. Primarily, I wish to thank my loving wife, Diane, who on Christmas of 2004, gave me a leather-bound journal. She encouraged me to write and thus wrestle with God through the monumental transitions and mounting losses of that year.

Initially I wrote only for myself, as a spiritual exercise. Through the following decade, it grew in an attempt to verbalize the sometimes-too-painful emotions of barbed blessings. I never intended these thoughts to be public, but I found in teaching and counseling that I was not alone in this condition of being without Eden. Through many, many, many edits and rewrites, Diane has continued to help me translate the ethereal of my mind into the words on these pages. Where any ideas remain elusive or obscure it is because I admittedly did not take her advice. Any and all confusing thoughts are mine alone.

This book is written as a result of our own field trips with Jesus, reflecting a Christ-centered voice. The insights, however, pertain to anyone's spiritual pilgrimage, and I fully intend to be inclusive of spirituality in general. Seeking truth and living in grace and communion during our exile are the privilege and hope of all.

Thank you also to our children, Chris, Hilary, Byron, Colin, and Letebrhan, and extended family for patience, for reading, for critique and work on the cover design, and for believing my heart. Kudos to Riley, David, Ruth, Kristen, Dan, and Dad Voetmann. Thanks to Dave Brenner, who in the final stretch added depth. To Steve and Ginny Saint, words fail to speak my gratitude for the kindness and courage you have shown to me and Diane as, together, we seek the radiant joy of Jesus.

There are many in Sudan, Yemen, Jordan, Israel and the West Bank whose lives have enriched ours in immeasurable ways. Some, for their own safety, must remain nameless. Of those I can name, Francis Kenyi, Yual Yual, Yusef, true brothers in the faith, you carry the scars of Christ. Thank you for all you have taught me about nurturing an eternity-based perspective of the goodness of God, irrespective of life's shifts and turmoil, and as importantly, about hearing and believing his whispered good news through silence. "Ar-Rab as-salah, kul al-waqt. All the time, God is good." Great is your reward in Heaven.

From Ethiopia, I am deeply appreciative of Vicki, Claire, Romil, and William and Alemzehai who, together in Aksum, sought the good within a very dark corner. Dearest Brother and Sister, as you walk the valley of shadows, know God is kindling his dawn. Our deep love and prayers continue with you. My gratitude and deep respect also go to Kudus, Aregawi, Tom, Lynn, and Ellen—friends who have graciously enriched our lives and that of our children.

I raise a toast to the Gun Beach crew on Guam, whose gathering reflects inclusiveness and grace. Each, in unique ways, has helped me weave together disparate thoughts, encouraging me along the way to persevere, to seek farther horizons and, like the navigators of old, to venture to distant shores. A special thanks to the Patron Saint of the Islands, Bruce Best; the Guardian Angels of the Pacific skies and Guam's children, Suzanne and Dave Hendricks; Chronicler of Micronesian diving, Dianne Strong; as well as Boyd Dixon and Sandy Yee, whose support and trust allowed me to dig dirt and to explore truly rare beauty that few ever see.

And a final, special thanks to Doreen Button for her initial editing, and to Teresa Ortiz and the entire Stonebridge team who provided invaluable editing and questions, adding clarity and fluidity to an admittedly heavy and sometimes rambling narrative.

Prologue

As a doe longs for running streams,
so longs my soul for you, my God.
My soul thirsts for God, the God of life;
when shall I go to see the face of God?

Deep is calling to deep as your cataracts roar;
all your waves, your breakers, have rolled over me.

Psalm 42:1-2, 7 JB

Like the Psalmist, there may come a day in our faith-walk when we rise, still shaken from a storm-tossed, horror-filled night, or possibly stand bereft over the splintered shards of our shattered dreams, or hear uttered that diagnosis which severs the last few web-thin threads that so tenuously held hope within our breaking hearts. Life comes crashing down around our heads and we seek for an answer, any answer, as to what remains of our supposed faith in this God we thought we knew so much about.

How we hunger for a glimpse of the God we once knew, and to revel again in his goodness. How we thirst for his once-known rest and reassurance. How we long for redemption, restoration, resurrection.

The promises we triumphantly used to claim in God are the very promises that now seem to mock us. We languish, feeling forsaken within the clangor of our calamities. Like Adam and Eve, we now view his once-perfect creation through a topsy-turvy, upside-down, locked-out, ruined state.

Whereas once God walked with us in the cool of the day, now the clang of Eden's gates hauntingly echoes in our ears. Images fill our heads; the Shepherd-God, our loving Father, the tender Bridegroom, our Deliverer, victoriously riding on the clouds. Through it all, however, often instead of salvaging our failures or fixing our problem, God remains silent.

Now disconsolate, we may feel betrayed, lost, exiled, and utterly alone. Wave after wave, breaker upon breaker of God's deep rolls over us, and in piercingly new ways, in ways previously unknowable, we awake to the undeniable reality that we live far removed from Eden. And dejectedly we endure, still nowhere near to God's intended Eternity. Seeking hard after a God guised in such silence, there dawns a disquieting sense that it is *his* peace, *his* stillness, *his* calm which is about to become our storm. How should we continue to seek amidst such solitude?

Because a health-n-wealth, culturally-biased Christianity has subtly seeped into our understanding of God and his word, the long periods of this apparent silence can increasingly feel like parental neglect, abandonment, or something even far worse. Seeking God within this isolation might seem an empty exercise. We need repeatedly to be reminded, heartened, that within *his* ever-seeking compassion, God does hear, he does care for, and he does love us in radical ways, mysterious ways, God-ways. Herein is good news.

In God's infinite wisdom and correcting, healing-kindness, he waits longingly, lovingly to whisper his intimate, relevant answer to each one of us through this, our punctuated, pained wilderness wanderings from Eden. Jesus forewarned us,

"In this world you will have hardship, but be courageous: I have conquered the world."

John 16:33 JB

And then he went forth to be crucified.

God knows we have lost our way. When we were expelled from Eden, God, as Emmanuel, also placed himself on our side of that clanged-shut gate. It is he who is seeking us.

What's more, we are not pledged simply a return to Paradise. Amazingly, we are instead promised an eternal embrace within God's everlasting Home.

WHEN WE WERE EXPELLED FROM EDEN, GOD, AS EMMANUEL, ALSO PLACED HIMSELF ON OUR SIDE OF THAT CLANGED-SHUT GATE. IT IS HE WHO IS SEEKING US.

When one dares enter into the deeper, fuller elements of relationship with the Eternal, our Love-Divine, simplistic answers no longer suffice. There are no quick fixes. Assuredly, at times God seems distant, even neglectful, but this, only because his ultimate answers are far more expansive and of such deeper magnitude than the thin-minded questions we continually ask.

God is bold. He is brash. But rest assured, God knows what he's about.

GOD IS BOLD. HE IS BRASH. BUT REST ASSURED, GOD KNOWS WHAT HE'S ABOUT.

---

adam without eden

HOPE FAR FROM HOME

It Is Well with My Soul

When peace, like a river, attendeth my way,
when sorrows like sea billows roll;
whatever my lot, thou hast taught me to say,
It is well, it is well with my soul.

Though Satan should buffet, though trials should come,
let this blest assurance control,
that Christ has regarded my helpless estate,
and hath shed his own blood for my soul.

And, Lord, haste the day when my faith shall be sight,
the clouds be rolled back as a scroll;
the trump shall resound, and the Lord shall descend,
even so, it is well with my soul.

Horatio G. Spafford

Chapter 1

Get in the Boat

Bad news never takes a day off.

Several decades back while studying in Jerusalem, I would frequent the rarely visited Protestant cemetery on Mt. Zion. On one of my initial explorations, just to the right as I passed through the rusted, wrought-iron gate, I noticed a common grave. Its headstone silently listed the names of those too poor to afford their individual six feet of earth. In the left column, several names down, I stopped reading, recognizing the name Horatio G. Spafford, the author of the noted hymn. Later, I discovered the story behind the hymn.

Over a century earlier, having sent his family on ahead for a much-needed European vacation, Spafford received a telegram from his wife, "Saved alone." All four of their pre-adolescent daughters perished when their vessel, struck mid-Atlantic by another ship, sank. This tragedy followed on the footfalls of the death of their only son to scarlet fever two years previous and the Great Chicago Fire that destroyed most of his real estate investments.

Spafford's church, believing these to be divine punishments, rejected him. Only then could he write such a hymn. Still seeking the face of God, he moved the remnant of his family to the Holy Land, establishing the American

Colony in Jerusalem. There, insanity eventually rested its cruel chaos upon his mind. By the end of his life he truly believed himself to be a messianic figure, but not before he had penned one final verse.

SPAFFORD HAD A GOOD TEACHER. HE KNEW JESUS ALONE TO BE MORE THAN SUFFICIENT.

"For me, be it Christ, be it Christ hence to live: If Jordan above me shall roll, No pain shall be mine, for in death as in life Thou shalt whisper Thy Peace to my soul."

Upon his death, his body was laid in a common grave.

Spafford had a good teacher. He knew Jesus alone to be more than sufficient.

Almost two thousand years before, on Passover eve, word comes to Jesus that his cousin, John the Baptizer, has been murdered over something as trite as a drunken birthday bash gone wrong. The licentious Herod Antipas, lusting over his niece/stepdaughter's sensual dancing had promised her anything, up to half the kingdom. "What should I ask for, Mummy? Tell me. Tell meeee!" Thus was uttered the order that the head of God's final prophet be parted from his body and brought to the little vixen on a silver platter.

Wake up to news like that and you know you're going to have a rough day of it, even if you are the Son of God.

Passover is a celebration, the commemoration of a birthday of sorts. It allows his people the time necessary to reflect upon the long gestational period of slavery in Egypt, the bleeding out of the sacrificial lamb, the breaking of the Red Sea's water, and the forty-year labor in the wilderness. The Exodus event marks the birthing of the nation. It is also called the feast of unleavened bread, the significance of which we will soon appreciate more fully.

On this, of all days, bad news comes knocking. The disciples scrutinize Jesus to observe his answer. Having now lived with him for about a year, they know it won't be conventional. They have yet to live with him long enough, however, to recall that he is always in control.

Imagine it. Put yourself there.

"Psst, Peter, ask him what he's going to do?"

"Why do you guys keep pestering me?"

Jesus, with a sad smile says, "Relax guys, who's up for a field trip?"

Twelve sets of eyes squint in a vain attempt toward comprehension.

"Did Jesus just say 'field trip'?"

"Gentlemen, get in the boat."

Life has a nasty habit of slapping us awake with bad news. We look to Jesus for answers, but instead of comforting us or fixing the problem, he suggests a field trip? Repeatedly, as our day descends from the horrible to the deplorable, we will hear his command, "get in the boat." With Jesus at the helm, we find ourselves not running from our problems. No, we are running straight into them, full throttle, through a maelstrom of shattered dreams, life threatening storms, and living nightmares far worse than the imagined ones ever could be.

Jesus knew this day would come. It was part of the plan, but it still holds extreme pain. Something has changed. Something new is afoot, something subtle. The old order of things has run its course. There are no loud, clanging bells or neon lights pointing it out, but the death of John the Baptizer is the swan song for the Old Testament—the culmination of all things past, ushering in a new era, the nativity of the kingdom come.

Earlier Jesus, in Luke 7:28, had said it himself, "Of all the children born of women, a greater than John the Baptizer has never been seen; yet the least in the new kingdom of heaven, is greater than he is." (Author's paraphrase)

Welcome to the Jesus Kingdom.

Jesus strongly desires instructional time with his disciples to prep them for all that this new covenant entails. From now on it is going to be intensive field trips, learning with the Master.

Climb aboard on this Jesus field trip as Jesus shuttles his crew to the far side of the Sea of Galilee, to a deserted place, far from the maddening multitudes for some much needed downtime of quiet reflection. The shore we disembark upon, however, is littered with a disease-stricken, hodgepodge of a crowing crowd.

And he has compassion on them.

Jesus' immediate need for quiet reflection takes a back seat to the new demands of the kingdom come. By now, however, along with the disciples, we have ceased watching Jesus for answers. Our focus is only on the bunch of local yokels who have crashed our party.

As our day wears thin, the horde, having had their medical needs attended to, turns hungry for more of the physical. "Send them off to buy bread," the disciples demand of Jesus.

"You give them bread," Jesus replies.

Philip, the local Bethsaida boy pipes up, "We're pretty far from any bakery, and since it's right before the Passover and all, no one's got any bread anyway, and even if we could buy bread it would be like, two hundred silver denarii or more so, yeah, you get where I'm coming from, right?"

Andrew, wanting to prove he's got it more together, interjects, "There's a kid here with five rock-hard lumps of barley bread and a couple of fish fingerlings." Awareness dawns as he scans the thousands. "Not really sure why I would mention that though." He slumps back into the disconcerted band of ill-prepared disciples.

Jesus draws in a long breath as he looks the crowd over before settling his gaze upon his crew. "Relax, I got this." What results is one of the few stories that shows up in all four gospel accounts. Jesus blesses the food, feeds to overflowing five thousand men, in addition to the women and children, and there is just enough left over for each disciple to have a sack lunch for the following day. Now this is the way to launch a kingdom.

None of this is lost on the crowd, or the disciples. They all know John, *their* prophet, has just been beheaded. They clue into the fact that a miracle-working bread-giver has been talking about the Kingdom of Heaven.

They all labor under the double oppression of Rome and the Herods. Connecting the dots that it is Passover eve—the celebration of freedom from slavery—the variables in this equation clearly compute to the fact that Jesus really is the long-ago foretold prophet greater than Moses, David, and Solomon.

A kingdom needs a king of course. "King Jesus." Can you see the restrained smirks, the gleam in the disciples' eyes? "Gentlemen, we backed the right horse."

"Word." Everyone nods in unison. "You got that right."

"Get in the boat." Jesus commands.

"Say again, Boss?"

"Get in the boat. Now!" Jesus is stern.

"But . . . the kingdom . . . You're . . . not coming?"

"Boat! NOW!" he demands, his eyes flash hot.

Can you relate?

Hours later, still rowing, because the winds like everything else are against us, we, with the disciples, find ourselves alone in the middle of the lake hating our lives. It's dark. Terribly dark. Waves shudder and thud threateningly against the bow, when soon-to-be St. John finally asks, "What just happened back there?"

Definitely not-yet-St. Peter turns around with a scowl. "I'll tell you what just happened, genius boy. We were this close to the kingdom. We were going to have revival. No more stinking like fish. No more grunting it out on the waves. No more back talk from those prim little Pharisees and those so-sad Sadducees. We all were going to be the king's men." His voice cracks. "We were this close . . . and would have had it made."

Thomas chimes in, "I can't believe this is happening. I just can't believe it."

"Well at least we didn't have to pay for that fiasco," Judas Iscariot adds, tapping the money bag for good measure.

"Is this not like the worst day of our lives, or what? What a ripoff of a field trip."

"Thanks for that, Philip."

"What? I'm just saying, okay? It's not like things can get any worse. Middle of the night, a raging storm, this Kingdom of Heaven gig nastily snatched from our grasp, rowing and getting nowhere. Dude."

Strange isn't it. We often think we've got God so figured out that when he does something contrary to our demands of him we get upset.

When Jesus walks away from our crowning him King of Kings amidst our shower of praise, we get offended. When he sends the lunch-filled and healed throng away during our calling fire down from heaven, our revival altar call, our moment of triumph, we question his commands.

The first 'get in the boat' we can understand. Jesus is with us, heading for a much needed retreat, and we then find ourselves at a coronation. "Cool!" We are finally going to figure out who this mystery man is. The second 'get in the boat,' we are ordered to leave just as all our dreams are coming true. And this time without him. Remember the Jesus Kingdom? What was that about?

The disciples obeyed that second command reluctantly, questioningly, doubtfully.

"Jesus must have flipped out. Isn't this whole 'Kingdom of Heaven thing' why we signed up for this gig in the first place? It's the first day of the Kingdom of Heaven and then when it actually happens, he tells us to get in the blasted boat. Who, in his name, does he think he is?"

Matthew, the Roman collaborator and outsider, finally chimes in, "Gentlemen, I believe it just got worse."

It's true. Intermittent flashes of lightning illuminate a specter coming right for us, unwaveringly walking atop the waves. Chills plunk a pallid score upon the xylophone of our collective spine. Thunder percusses. In unison, everyone yells, "Phantom!"

The disciples having obeyed out of doubt rather than faith, are focusing on the waves, the storm, the fact that God has just ripped them off. And then they ask who Jesus thinks he is. Yeah, it just got worse.

Mystifying. When we forget God's enormity and the fact that his kingdom is not of this earth, we mistake our only hope, our only salvation, with something ephemeral, an apparition, or even a lie. The only answer left to us, that God is God and we are not, becomes our deepest dread, imbuing us with a sense of the imminent destruction of our faith and the end of all we hold sacred.

STRANGE ISN'T IT. WE OFTEN THINK WE'VE GOT GOD SO FIGURED OUT THAT WHEN HE DOES SOMETHING CONTRARY TO OUR DEMANDS OF HIM WE GET UPSET.

Because we lose focus of whom the King of the Kingdom actually is, we perceive Jesus, striding toward us, walking on the tumultuous waves amidst life's worst storms, to be a defiling phantom, a nightmare, our worst fears incarnate.

Like the disciples, we may only reluctantly be in Jesus' boat, obeying out of fear rather than devotion. Yet that is still a measure of obedience. Yes, the storms still rage, both physical and spiritual, and then Jesus, walking on the water, gives us a new set of commands, "Stop fearing. Start believing."

Jesus, having sought us out, then gets into our boat. He comes alongside us and, holding our hands tenderly as a father would a lost, frightened child's, helps us to obey, this time in faith. The storm ceases, placid, calmed, stilled. As he did for Spafford, he speaks peace to our soul.

"So, how was the field trip?" Jesus asks his disciples.

Together, awestruck, we answer that last question so arrogantly asked earlier, the one about who he thought he was. This time, however, from a different, a renewed, right-way-up understanding.

Jesus fashions a new mental landscape, a shifting of our understandings, not only of himself, but of our world.

"Truly, you are the Son of the living God."

Jesus smiles. "Good, then gear up. Our next field trip is to those tombs on that far pagan shore to meet up with a naked, legion-possessed, demoniac of a raving lunatic. And look, we're already in the boat and each has a packed lunch this time. Man, is this great, or what?"

JESUS FASHIONS A NEW MENTAL LANDSCAPE, A SHIFTING OF OUR
UNDERSTANDINGS, NOT ONLY OF HIMSELF, BUT OF OUR WORLD.

Surprised by Joy

Surprised by joy—impatient as the Wind
I turned to share the transport—Oh! with whom
But Thee, long buried in the silent Tomb,
That spot which no vicissitude can find?
Love, faithful love, recalled thee to my mind—
But how could I forget thee?—Through what power,
Even for the least division of an hour,
Have I been so beguiled as to be blind
To my most grievous loss!—That thought's return
Was the worst pang that sorrow ever bore,
Save one, one only, when I stood forlorn,
Knowing my heart's best treasure was no more;
That neither present time, nor years unborn
Could to my sight that heavenly face restore.

William Wordsworth

Chapter 2

An Anguishing Why

Joy – delirious and sudden – surprised Wordsworth awake. Turning to share it with his beloved, with his "heart's best treasure," he found only the empty, pointlessness of a child's tomb. Awakened to the dreadful shock that a moment had passed wherein he did not carry the pain of his loss, he penned this poem.

The gospel carries another story of empty, pointless death, multifold. We call it the slaughter of the innocents. Living five years within the simmering hostility of occupied Bethlehem with a two-year-old son, my wife, Diane and I became acutely aware that had we lived in Jesus' day, our son would have been the target of an assassin's blade. Such a travesty is scarcely imaginable.

Faint rumblings pulse to thunder. Within a moment the hoof-beats of a hundred horses shatter the pre-dawn as Roman soldiers quickly surround Bethlehem, cutting off all roads in or out. Herod's militiamen, consulting parchments, bark commands to their underlings. Half a hundred brutal-looking men, two men per unit, swords drawn, maraud through the early dawn streets, fully armed.

Sleep rudely, rapaciously is ripped from bodies as heavily shod feet come crashing, splintering through feeble doors. Screams of terror and outrage mingle with shouts and curses. Families huddle in the back of their small dwellings. Hate invades their private space, snatching an infant from his mother's breast. A sword flashes dull silver, blinks and bleeds red. Thud. And the fiend vanishes.

Hell has paid a visit to Bethlehem.

Time trickles like cold blood. One, two, three, . . . heart beats labor on . . . six, seven.

Judgment Day is turned on its head. Innocent children summarily slaughtered and the wealthy oppressors rejoice. All lucidity crumbles under the heat of Herod's madness.

A father lumbers from his mat. Has it been a minute, an hour, an eternity? Staggering, he gropes his way toward his fractured door which hangs from one remaining leather hinge. He trips over an object that feels like rags enveloping a doughy lump. Silver morning sunlight meekly steals through that shattered portico. He looks. At his feet, still and pale, lies their child, serenely quiet, haloed in his own precious blood.

A mother rocks back and forth, mewling in an upright fetal position. Moans and deep anguish plummet then ricochet up from the million-stadia's depth of her anguished soul. Such depths are plumbed in an instant. And what life still pulses in her, groans and utters words of a universally spoken, yet unintelligible, language.

Another father sinks to his knees beside his son's lifeless, infant body. He pets the quiet corpse as if deliberately touching fire. The magnitude of his pain and loss hits him. With clenched white-knuckled fists he covers his eyes as he screams, then supplicates, then sobs. Words fail to speak the language of the broken heart; only primal utterances are listed in that lexicon.

All around, giant Satanic shadows play the soldiers like marionettes. Hideous laughter echoes across the heavens. Impudent spirits gesture and scoff at the heavenly warriors hovering above the melee. They have been given strict orders not to intervene. Dark, oily beings spit and curse at the heavenly hosts who easily outnumber them. The only Heaven-ones allowed in are the massive opalescent guardians. These place house-sized hands over each slaughtered infant, crushing any vile Shadow foolish enough to come near. As with all his creations, these minuscule souls are precious to the KING. None shall cradle them but the KING Himself.

"Enough!" shakes the heavens. All stops mid-motion. "Depart!" All Shadows sulk away, beaten mongrels. The Heaven-ones shut their eyes and turn their heads as burning light envelopes them. The Great KING sighs, "Come, best beloved!" Exuberant light sparkles from these many faceted gems, these slaughtered innocents, as they fall up into heaven's embrace.

Heaven's armies stand at attention as the KING retakes His throne.

Southwest of all such horror and warfare, an exhausted man dressed in Galilean garb, with his wife and newborn son, refugees astride a donkey, amble down a desolate road toward Egypt. No strangers pass. Their only companions consist of twelve legions of Heaven's mightiest Warriors.

Yet not many weeks prior the heavens had rung with angelic triumph,

> *"Glory to God in the highest heaven, and peace to men who enjoy his favor."*
>
> Luke 2:14 JB

At such times, no answer intelligible to our fallen humanity suffices. Even seeking solace in the Psalms offers cold comfort.

> *"Why, Yahweh, do you keep so distant, stay hidden in times of trouble? In his pride the wicked man hunts down the weak. In the undergrowth he lies in ambush, in his hiding-place he murders the innocent. He watches intently for the downtrodden."*
>
> Psalm 10:1-2a, 7b-8 NJB

How then is one to fathom the carnage of God's sovereignty?

For this, for so many of God's darker allowances, I have no answer. Like those in the Gospels who came to Jesus demanding an answer, I find that I have yet to ask the right questions. In the same way the empty tomb is a far more profound upending of the question that is the crucifixion, so the ultimate revelation of God's purpose is an inversion of our ways of knowing.

"Yahweh, you listen to the lament of the poor, you give them courage, you grant them a hearing, to give judgment for the orphaned and exploited, so that earthborn humans may strike terror no more."

Psalm 10: 17-18 NJB

Beginning our faith-walk, innocent as babes in Christ, the freshly forgiven heart pursues the unfathomable mysteries of God with the heady exuberance of a cherub chasing the rainbow's end. We know God to only be good. He has saved us. We live within the triumph of Good News.

So assured of this are we, we can taste it. Sunsets sing out our praise. Our conscience squeaks clean, while the beautiful scent of salvation permeates every cranny of our once-fetid soul. We breathe it in, this grandeur of God, knowing deeply that magnitude of his love. Daily we walk the pleasant glades of God's paradise in wonderment, glorying in the goodness of this God. All our field trips are fun. Everywhere, in everything, God's loving-kindness rings true.

And then?

Imperceptibly at first, as faith matures, we discern that life's rains are not always gentle or refreshing. Dark storms loom where no rainbows exist. Old hymns about rugged crosses and billowing waves of sorrows begin to hold more bearing than do happy tunes abounding in the gushy love of God. Or even more faith-threatening, our garden chats with the "dew still on the roses" seem less intimate, more stilted. The cadence of our once-infatuated prayers takes on the monotone of a too-comfortable, too-tired couple simply going through the motions on Tuesday's dinner date.

Behind us lies Eden.

On our horizon, deserts loom, a famine of the word of God threatens. Like the disciples in John six, we long for a truth that is less demanding, a boat secured within safe harbors, a Savior more accommodating to our beliefs. But where else can we go? Upon whom else can we trust? God owns the monopoly on eternal life.

We may question that initial goodness. Feeling betrayed, alone, lied to, we search his words, his love letters to us. Reclaiming promises like Jeremiah 29 with a "future and a hope" and plans for prosperity and such, we find they seem now only to mock us. Hoping to woo him back into love with us, we pour our hearts out to him. We serve more fervently. We begin to seek deeper answers. Our words wear tears.

Until one day, we briefly wake to a joy we wish to share with God and are struck with palpable silence. Turning around, expecting to see God running toward us penitent and conciliatory, we instead are shocked to discover, like Adam and Eve, the clanged-shut gates to Paradise, with us locked out and on the wrong side.

Panic and bewilderment inform our scattered minds that, yes, even as God's precious bride-to-be, lost, afraid, and broken, we reside in occupied territory under the cruel and hateful dominion of that vile serpent, Satan. Who then is there to lift us out of our grief, comfort us, and whisper that we indeed are loved and not alone?

> A FAMINE OF THE WORD OF GOD THREATENS. LIKE THE DISCIPLES IN JOHN SIX, WE LONG FOR A TRUTH THAT IS LESS DEMANDING, A BOAT SECURED WITHIN SAFE HARBORS, A SAVIOR MORE ACCOMMODATING TO OUR BELIEFS. BUT WHERE ELSE CAN WE GO? UPON WHOM ELSE CAN WE TRUST? GOD OWNS THE MONOPOLY ON ETERNAL LIFE.

Through Scripture, God reminds us, sometimes in a whisper, sometimes through his thunder, "Remember." He was there as the Alpha and he will see us through as the Omega. Before Adam and Eve were driven from Eden, God cut a covenant that a Second Adam, a promised one, would crush the serpent's head. Even the initial fulfillment of that promise, however, stood thousands of years off.

Herein begins the hardest work of exile – structuring faith by being still and knowing he is God. The first promise God made to Father Abraham, back when he was Abram, the childless refugee, was that God would make of him a great nation whereby all nations would be blessed. He was seventy-five years old.

"Some time later," we are told, God reiterates his promise. "Look upon the countless starry expanse. Such will your progeny be." In faith, Abram believes in the long-obedience, and this is reckoned to him as righteousness.

At eighty-five, however, Abram is still waiting for the promise. Sarai, his seventy-five-year-old, barren wife speaks, "God gave you a promise, right? Name it and claim it! He helps those who help themselves. Show some initiative." And thus was born to him his son, of a slave. The child is given the ironic name, "It is God who hears."

Then, when Abram is ninety-nine, God again makes a visit. "Remember that promise?"

Abram smiles, looks over at his son affectionately and says, "Yeah, thanks for that."

"I've come to fulfill it."

Abram, an eyebrow raised states, "Say what?"

"You are now Abraham, father of many nations. The son I promised you, your only begotten son of the promise, will be born from ninety-year-old Sarai, who henceforth will be Sarah, and you will know it is God who provides." Millennia had passed before the original promise to Adam was reiterated to Abraham.

Even within Abraham's part of this epic drama, it took two and a half decades for God's initial stage of his promise to finally be fulfilled. It took another four centuries for Abraham's progeny to escape slavery in Egypt and begin owning the promise of a 'promised land.' Another twelve hundred years would pass before the fulfillment of all the covenants through the provision of the true seed of Abraham, the "Only begotten Son of the promise."

Two thousand years on, we still wait the completion of a promise spoken to Adam and Eve over six thousand years ago. For as we read in Hebrews,

"All these died in faith, before receiving any of the things that had been promised, but they saw them in the far distance and welcomed them, recognizing that they were only strangers and nomads on earth. People who use such terms about themselves make it quite plain that they are in search of their real homeland."

Hebrews 11:13-14a JB

Consider then, Enoch and Noah, Abraham and Moses, David, Gideon, Jephthah, and Rahab. These all died in faith having not yet received the promise.

The reason given in Scripture is that this promise is a cumulative millennia-gathering of grace to include even us. As we will be, so they were, received into the embrace of their God of the promise.

He is walking this long road with us as Emmanuel, in the same way he walked with Abraham, Moses, and Jeremiah, or Debra, Hannah, and Mary. It is he who is walking us Home. We view Romans 8:28, where God brings together all things for good to those who love him, as true, but a truth yet to be completed within a God-intended, God-ordained time.

The sometimes decades-long silence of God draws upon our faith in ways nothing else ever will. But it is here we gradually learn to view and eventually embrace our more authentic God through a less fragile faith.

"From the beginning till now the entire creation, as we know, has been groaning in one great act of giving birth; and not only creation, but all of us who possess the first-fruits of the Spirit, we too groan inwardly as we wait for our bodies to be set free. For we must be content to hope that we shall be saved — our salvation is not in sight, we should not have to be hoping for it if it were — but, as I say, we must hope to be saved since we are not saved yet — it is something we must wait for with patience."

Romans 8:22-25 JB

Say what? "We must hope to be saved since we are not saved yet?" And I thought this whole signing on the dotted line thing, jumping through the hoops of the sinner's prayer, walking up to the front of the church at the altar call was my golden ticket, my guarantee of the good life, an assurance of salvation. Now I find I need to wait, like everyone else, for my salvation with patience.

THIS PROMISE IS A CUMULATIVE MILLENNIA-GATHERING OF GRACE TO INCLUDE EVEN US. AS WE WILL BE, SO THEY WERE, RECEIVED INTO THE EMBRACE OF THEIR GOD OF THE PROMISE.

As I read deeply, I find that just as creation is pregnant with the grandeur of God's intended new creation, groaning with labor pains, travailing under the burden of the fall, so are we pregnant with God's promise of salvation. Since in God there is no such thing as "before," there is no "and then." In God, we are saved.

"Only faith can guarantee the blessings that we hope for, or prove the existence of the realities that at present remain unseen."

Hebrews 11:1 JB

Our present reality is that our faith-walk is preparing us for a home we have never been to, nor if it were described to us could we even imagine. But first comes the labor, the hard work. It is called labor for a very real reason. Birth, joyful and freeing, is the long goal of pregnancy. The far less joyful pain and travail of labor are the means by which that child is pushed out into life.

Salvation then is our finally being birthed into Heaven as children of God. Our life here can be viewed as the gestational period for our spiritual life. Our existence, this constrained and lightless womb-world, does seem like suffering. But as St. Paul describes in II Corinthians 4:17, this spiritual exercise is preparing us, as does weight-training, to bear an age-to-age weight of glory.

I would never wish to make light of suffering. I have known far too many people who have suffered grievously at the hands of others. But St. Paul states that our sufferings here are light and momentary compared to the spiritual benefits received once we are full-term and birthed into Heaven.

Any dimension of suffering in my life, I acknowledge as small compared to so many others I have known, or of so many others around the world. I was born in what is now the war-ravaged country of the Democratic Republic of Congo. Of the six children born to missionary parents on that small station, I alone survived the ravaging of malaria, just barely. As a high-schooler, I visited the cemetery where once lay my already-dug grave. I wept for peers I never had the privilege to know.

Having both grown up in Africa, my wife Diane and I experienced the trauma of war from an early age. During the often-brutal struggle for independence across Africa, followed by the turmoil of nation-building, we observed man's injustice to man up close. Being near to the Ugandan border, my family was able to flee the 1964 Leninist-fed Simba rebellion in Congo. We escaped with few belongings and less than an hour to spare before being overrun. Other missionaries and many civilians, local Christians and ministers were massacred.

Diane's family lived on a mission hospital station in the mid 70s, during Zimbabwe's civil war. She recalls helicopters full of battle-bloodied soldiers; whispered conversations of rebel leaders in her house reassuring her father they would not shoot down his mission airplane because they knew he loved Africans; the day she and her sister were not blown up by a landmine, because another car, having passed minutes earlier, triggered its death instead.

With our own family, living in the Middle East, we have been on the receiving end of conflicts, with tanks rumbling outside our house, heavy munitions screaming down our street, and bullets coming through our bedroom windows. More than once we have had to pack up and be out of a country within less than a week. Undeniably, these "war stories" have weighed upon our development as children, and have emotionally and spiritually molded and shaped us as adults. Yet these reside as externals, on an entirely different plane than the deeply personal struggles and pains within the walls of our homes and families.

These are slight compared to the true suffering of those whom we have had the privilege of serving. Under blankets on the floor of the back seat of our car, while our two year old sweetly sang, we once smuggled a young Yemeni believer through military checkpoints because his life was forfeit for having found his Messiah. He hid in our home while waiting for asylum in the Netherlands.

We have known good friends martyred. We have worked intimately with African refugees. We have dear brothers who were imprisoned, tortured, and beaten for the gospel. We shared our home with a Sudanese brother whose wife was taken from him and given to another because he, even after being water-boarded over a period of six months and repeatedly scourged, still refused to deny Christ. He confided that he only wears long-sleeve shirts and long pants as his entire body is covered in scars from torture. Another friend is forced to move from place to place because, as a member of an Arab royal family whom Jesus has embraced, his life is threatened. I have discipled a leader of the Hamas youth brigade after he too had to go into hiding. These could be included in the Hebrews 11 list of the faithful.

As exiles out of Eden, barbed blessings are not exclusive to the developing world. Within our immediate and extended families here in the United States, we have been touched by death and cancer. And these, not only of grandparents, but the loss of a wife and mother of young children, a preschooler to spina bifida, miscarriages. We carry the living grief of disabilities and cognitive delay in children, divorce, childlessness, Alzheimer's, and the loss of jobs, businesses, and homes. And I would venture to say we are not far from the average American family in this measure of suffering and loss.

External and physical losses may readily be identified. Others, with a more subtle spiritual and emotional nature, lie hidden. Magnitudes of suffering cannot be compared. All weigh heavily upon our hearts, occasioning sleepless nights and deep anguish.

Throughout this book, my prayer remains that together we learn what God in his infinite wisdom and compassion is waiting to whisper to each of us amidst our brokenness and this silence of our yearning, our travail between our loss of

Eden and our being ushered into Heaven.

There is indeed only one Good Shepherd, and *he* is actively seeking after each one of us, his lost lambs. Storm tossed, he does remember we are shipwrecked, lost, alone, and at times, drowning in our own inadequacies. God may at times seem distant, but only because his ultimate, his grace-filled answers are far bigger than the questions our exile-based understandings allow.

When Jesus came the first time he took upon himself life's infirmities, sin's stain, our death. There now lives only one death, his. When Jesus comes the second time, it will be to usher his precious, Eden-exiled, lonely bride into his eternal, loving embrace. Imagine it, Home, safe, truly surprised by joy.

Be Still My Soul

Be still, my soul; the Lord is on thy side
Bear patiently the cross of grief or pain
Leave to thy God to order and provide
In every change He faithful will remain
Be still, my soul: thy best, thy heav'nly Friend
Thro' thorny ways leads to a joyful end.

Be still, my soul; thy God doth undertake
To guide the future as He has the past
Thy hope, thy confidence let nothing shake
All now mysterious shall be bright at last
Be still, my soul: the waves and wind still know
His voice who ruled them while he dwelt below.

Be still, my soul; the hour is hast'ning on
When we shall be forever with the Lord
When disappointment, grief, and fear are gone
Sorrow forgot, love's purest joys restored
Be still, my soul: when change and tears are past
All safe and blessed we shall meet at last.

Original - Katharina A. Von Schlegel, translated from the German
by Jane L. Borthwick

Chapter 3

Memory of God's Future

It was the second semester of my junior year at Westmont College, Santa Barbara, before I realized, in a very personal way, that God can deny one's heart's desire. Being a religious studies major who had grown up in East Africa as a missionary kid and because I still had contacts there, I was asked to co-lead a short-term mission trip for about twenty students. To my chagrin and utter embarrassment, the mission agency we selected to host us, without explanation, rejected me.

Wow. My first crisis of faith. At this tender age, it was as if God had broken up with me. We can probably all remember the raw, crystal-thin passions with coming of age. I recall the acute sensitivity and self-awareness of identity formation as I crafted my own faith from the instruction my parents had instilled. The fragility and first-shattering of my emerging spiritual passion, with the loss of some of its naivety, was just as transformatory.

In seeking solace, I would occasionally retreat to the small campus chapel and, starting at number one, play hymns on the piano to pour my heart out to God. And so hopefully woo him back into love with me.

I had grown up singing hymns, but it wasn't until I got to number 71 that the words stung me wide awake. *"Be still my soul; the Lord is on thy side."* Really? Isn't he the one who led me on with impassioned promises of a life-time call to the service of saving souls? And then when I stepped up, he slammed the once-opened door in my face, embarrassing me in front of my friends? Jesus had jilted me. I read on. *"Be still, my soul: thy best, thy heav'nly Friend thro thorny ways leads to a joyful end."* Are you serious?

In my life-long pilgrimage since, consisting of multiple crises of faith and other rejections, I have learned that, yes, God is deathly serious about his loving us. Look again at the words of this hymn and ask, what depth of grief and joy, heartache and passion could lead a woman to write these words? The second person I wish to embrace when I get to heaven is a lady I have never met named Katharina A. Von Schlegel, for her words, wept out into a hymn, have been my anthem ever since.

There have been and will be many more days when my hopes dwindle to dust. So dry and for so long have been some of life's droughts that at times I feared it would never rain blessings again. Yet drought, like fasting, takes my reliance off of me and my own ability to provide, and puts it back onto God.

At times I have pretended to know so much about God, and yet consider the percentage and scope of his infiniteness that remains outside of his revelation.

> *"Yes, the heavens are as high above earth as my ways are above your ways, my thought above your thoughts."*
> Isaiah 55:9 JB

Simplistic Sunday school answers no longer suffice, if indeed they ever could.

Within this stripping process, I encounter a God too big, a mystery too spiritual. My physicality precludes clearly seeing or accurately hearing the Divine. I am required to step out by faith, believing not seeing, believing not hearing. "Ay, there's the rub." Like St. Peter, in my eagerness to prove my reliance upon God, I follow Jesus with abandon. I venture out of the boat onto wind-swept waves. But life's storms awaken fear, and I begin to sink. During such dire straits, I seek to legitimate my fears.

The worst strain of fear is fear to hope. Fear and hope seem so counterintuitive, if not mutually exclusive. Fear constricts, leaving no place for hope, which is what makes it fear. Hope abides above the domain of fear, which is why it is hope.

Yet a fear to hope is a very real place in the human heart. The disciples felt it when a crazed Mary crashed her way into their dreadful, secluded self-doubt with news she had seen the risen Christ. Peter felt it when he joined Jesus for a post-resurrection fish breakfast on the shores of Galilee. "Peter, do you love me?"

So many have known the fear to hope, it seems to be the Bible's characterization of humanity's pilgrimage from Eden to Home. Adam and Eve, Noah, Abraham and Sarah, Jacob, Joseph, Moses, Hannah, David, Hezekiah, all the prophets, each at times, were afraid to hope. They knew God was able—that was never in question—but was he willing? That was the fear.

Mount Carmel without fire. Mount Sinai without the law. Mount of Olives without the return.

The spiritual pilgrimage, our Jesus field trips, are designed to take us out of fear and into hope. The fear to hope far too often is a natural place in the human heart. We've all been there. Moving away from fear and further into hope is a supernatural happening. We are all invited to be there instead.

I ENCOUNTER A GOD TOO BIG, A MYSTERY TOO SPIRITUAL. MY PHYSICALITY PRECLUDES CLEARLY SEEING OR ACCURATELY HEARING THE DIVINE. I AM REQUIRED TO STEP OUT BY FAITH.

When it comes to seeking answers within the realm of hope, never trust a disciple who has not suffered, for his or her solutions are governed by gold and security. And with God, there is neither. Remember the Psalms. Remember the Prophets. Remember Hebrews 11.

Hard and sharp are the promises of God. They cut where only he can heal. They rip what only he can mend. They crush and no one can stand. And this he declares his love. This he calls true life. God willingly, methodically strips us bare of our self-importance and then proceeds to scourge us. He leaves us nothing of our self-righteousness, what we once relied upon outside of him. Like a thief he pilfers us of our very sense of being. Like a swindler he cheats us out of our self-sufficiency. And then he invites us to embrace him in love.

This seemingly paradoxical, cruel heart of God dictates we should feel blessed by our wounds, and actively, willingly relinquish our life. Read the Gospels. Read of the crucifixion.

"My God, my God, why have you deserted me?"

Matthew 27:46 JB

Sound familiar? He abandons his Only Son of the Covenant, leaving him destitute and alone. And after all this, God allows Christ's enemies to dance upon his grave. He has the audacity to do these very things unto his Christ, so that in his flesh, he can live as our Emmanuel.

And thus we can live within our only and most profound hope; *"Christ in us, the hope of glory"* (Colossians 1:27 KJV). Amazing!

Hope, then, becomes the memory of God's future for us. Confidently we can look to this future, knowing God is already there. We live in the hope that what he said and promised is already accomplished. As we traverse time, God *is* in his heaven already abiding. With God there is no passage of time. It is we who need to be reminded of what God has already done, is doing right now, and will do for us in the future, which is why we are commanded,

"Do this in remembrance of me."

Luke 22:19 KJV

Why?

"Thus proclaiming the Lord's death and resurrection until he returns."

1 Corinthians 11:26 KJV

The point here is that Christ has already done all the heavy lifting. We walk now not only in faith but also in this most amazing and profound hope, all within this deep assurance—God's finale has already been composed. But because we are bound by time and space, it simply is taking us longer to hear it.

HOPE, THEN, BECOMES THE MEMORY OF GOD'S FUTURE FOR US. CONFIDENTLY WE CAN LOOK TO THIS FUTURE, KNOWING GOD IS ALREADY THERE.

In Colossians 3 we read that in God's context, we already are seated with Christ in the heavenlies where we are already proclaiming the truth that he is the beginning and the end, the alpha and omega, the author of faith. We live in confidence that when, from the cross, Jesus declared in John 19:30, *"it is finished"* fully, perfectly completed, he knew what he was talking about.

Hope is the assurance that what is future is accomplished now in God's present tense. As we are reminded,

"I am quite confident that the One who began a good work in you will go on completing it until the Day of Jesus Christ comes."

Philippians 1:6 NJB

And herein is the greatest promise of that hope—*"Peace I leave with you."* In John 14:27 we find that Jesus does not divvy out his peace when needed. It is already here, and he leaves it—*for us.*

Peace, the same peace that slept storm-tossed through the waves. The same peace that unshakably conversed with the pagan, naked, legion-possessed man. The same peace that marched into the temple and straight-armed the sellers of temporal solutions.

If we were truly able to walk in this peace, unafraid of the simple-minded reasons to fear, we would, like Jesus, contentedly rest through life's storms, confront the maniacal legions of our day, and overthrow the tables of our mediocre church doings and monkey-on-the-pony shows we so often claim as our service to him.

Peace is God walking in the Garden of Eden in the cool of the day, searching for our lost, frightened, shattered, hidden humanity and then barring the gates so that he would have to suffer the indignity of becoming Emmanuel, not only in time, but for all eternity, so that he might love a people devoid of love for him.

Peace is Jesus walking into the funeral of a twelve year old girl and stating, *"Little lamb, arise!"* Peace is Christ singing, while on the cross, the 22nd Psalm in its entirety, surrounded by his mortal enemies, slowly suffocating to death in his own failing incarnated flesh. Peace is Jesus walking straight up to Satan, his nail-pierced hand outstretched, and demanding the keys to Death and Hell.

This is a deathly serious peace. This peace, paradoxically, comes to bring a sword. This peace divides the living from the gangrene. This peace looks death in the face and declares, "Is that all you've got?" This peace turns an unjust, violent, cruel crucifixion into God's ultimate victory over Sin and Death. This peace initiates the tortuous process of reversing our catastrophes, upturning our world, reverting it to right-side up.

This is the peace we have. This is the peace that will make wars cease, for this peace is not simply the cessation of violence; it is the violence of cessation. It quietly, definitively puts to rest all rebellions, arguments, debates, discussions. It calms the storms, frees the occupied and possessed, and cleanses the temple.

The violence of this peace will shake and bring to ruin the false images we have made. It will desecrate the trivial shrines we so fastidiously maintain. God will stand upon this earth, and his peace will shatter what little peace we've hammered together out of fear of man, political expediency, and tepid devotions.

Peace is the deeply abiding presence of God, despite the depravity and the meaninglessness, the futility and conniving of all our religiosity. Peace is God sitting on his throne knowing that all our doubts, fears, accusations, excuses, and insipid Churchianity will dissipate like early morning mist before his returning glory.

Far and away then, the greatest gift of God is his abiding peace, an incarnational peace, born of confidence that despite the brokenness of our exile from Eden, God's promised deliverance is already accomplished.

Thus might we dwell, enfolded within Jesus' powerful peace, cognizant it is more akin to the eye of a storm than a quaint pastoral scene. Storms still will rage, storms that stretch every sinew of our faith. But with Christ in our boat, we can rest assured, *"the waves and wind still know His voice who ruled them while he dwelt below."*

Scripture is pregnant with promises, full of heaven, brimming with blessings. Through life's storms or amidst his long silence, his peace, our hope-fulfilled memory of God's future, is gravid with our yet-to-be glory.

> THE GREATEST GIFT OF GOD IS HIS ABIDING PEACE, AN INCARNATIONAL PEACE, BORN OF CONFIDENCE THAT DESPITE THE BROKENNESS OF OUR EXILE FROM EDEN, GOD'S PROMISED DELIVERANCE IS ALREADY ACCOMPLISHED.

"Peace I leave with you. My peace."

The Shaking of the Foundations

Time is our destiny. Time is our Hope. Time is our despair. And time is the mirror in which we see eternity. Let me point to three of the many mysteries of time: its power to devour anything within its sphere; its power to receive eternity within itself; and its power to drive toward an ultimate end, a new creation.

Paul Tillich

Chapter 4

Shipwrecked in Time

When God sings his finale, it will end time in the way we have come to know it. But a new kind of time, a different species of time, in a new and different age, awaits us far beyond where we live and what we can know right now. As this, our diseased age, limps toward its inevitable conclusion, we can either grasp frantically to what little remains for us here, or we can run freely, joyfully to an age where all things now will be inconsequential, forgotten shadows.

Despite our devotion and passion we sometimes find ourselves floundering in the Sea that is God. Like St. Peter, we focus upon the waves and winds of life's storms. Our inability to walk on water no longer in doubt, we cry out, *"Lord, save me!"*

I thought I had faith. I was simply believing, wasn't I? Jesus invited me to get out of the boat and walk on water with him. And then, through obedience, I find myself in deathly peril? Why does Jesus repeatedly act contrary to my expectations of him?

In one of the Bernstain Bears stories, Brother climbs into a box. Before long he is surprised to find himself loaded, upside down on a truck bouncing down the road to town. With one bump too many, he tumbles off. Running home, he excitedly declares, "Mommy, Mommy, I went to town, inside, outside, upside down." Now while this children's book teaches prepositions, it also illustrates our present reality.

We think we have apprehended God, incognizant that we live locked inside our simplistic, limited ways of knowing. Banished, we struggle now outside of God's perfect design. Bumped and bruised, we find ourselves injured, dizzy within a world turned violently upside down.

Jesus comes alongside and gently guides us towards correctly discerning our truer identity in him. "Stop fearing! Start believing! Keep your eyes on me!" With Jesus, we learn that crucifixion is victory, his peace brings a sword, the first will be last, and the meek will inherit the Earth, along with Heaven.

He reassures us of his unfailing faithfulness, and focuses us on the fact that one day, in his right-side-up kingdom, we shall see him face-to-face and know him as he already fully knows us.

As an archaeologist, I have held palm-sized, ancient Roman mirrors made from highly polished bronze. In a maritime city like Corinth, such mirrors needed constant polishing. By using a small sponge and a pumice powder abrasive, one might literally, just keep a day ahead of a tarnished image. Corinth was a pretentious city, projecting an image of urbane sophistication and unbridled tolerance. Looking good mattered far more than actually being good.

The Corinthian church grew infatuated with itself in terms of its identity and self-importance. By viewing their warped image of themselves as the icon reflecting what constituted "church", they thought they were doing God a favor.

Corinth was particularly known for its mirror production, so when St. Paul writes to the Corinthians that we see only a dim reflection of our truer selves and the world around us, they know well what he is talking about. Even looking intently in such a mirror, one glimpses merely hazy shadows and distorted refractions.

St. Paul provides us a brilliant example of what that looks like.

> *"For our knowledge is imperfect and our prophesying is imperfect; but once perfection comes, all imperfect things will disappear. When I was a child, I used to talk like a child, and think like a child, and argue like a child, but now I am a man, all childish ways are put behind me. Now we are seeing a dim reflection in a mirror; then we shall be seeing face-to-face. The knowledge that I have now is imperfect; but then I shall know as fully as I am known."*
> I Corinthians 13:9-13 JB

God has a supremely accurate, trans-temporal sense of clarity and a sharp, single-minded focus when it comes to knowing you and me. He does stop; he does stare. Amazingly, even mind-bendingly, what he sees in each one of us is so much more than the simple icon of our being made in his image.

God looks past our failures, beyond our fallenness, through his forgiveness, and actually sees his own reflection, unobscured, triumphantly emerging from all that still attempts to hold him in the tomb. The startling truth is, God views us now through the stark brilliance of Christ's resurrection, our true, God-bestowed, perfected identity. Again and again we need to remind ourselves of this aspect of our timeless, loving God.

Our view of God, however, is obscured. God is not lost. God does not hide, but through focus on our lostness and pain as the tempests roll, we can lose clear sight of his face. Measuring the goodness of God reflected in the dim, scratched surface of our mirror, renders a distorted, imperfect icon. In faith, seeking the face of God unobscured becomes the task of each believer.

As we have seen, not many gained the promises of God here in the land of shattered shadows, and the "faith people" of Hebrews 11 who did, still desired God more than his goodies. They, like Spafford, knew that to have God and nothing else is sufficient.

MEASURING THE GOODNESS OF GOD REFLECTED IN THE DIM, SCRATCHED SURFACE OF OUR MIRROR, RENDERS A DISTORTED, IMPERFECT ICON.

Like those heroes of the faith, I want to desire God, not just his promises. My genuine passion for God, however, often becomes subservient to my will for less of the requisite pain in getting him. Unfortunately, that's not the way it works, is it? Wanting God, one gets the suffering as well. *"I want to know Christ and the power of his resurrection,"* we happily quote. That is all well and good – but that knowledge comes with a price. Read further.

To know Christ and live within that resurrection power, one must first, as it continues in Philippians 3:10, *"partake in his sufferings by being moulded to the pattern of his death"* (NJB). There is no alternative. There can be no resurrection without death. That is what the Jesus field trips are designed to teach us.

Purposely looking into the face of God and seeing his pain and tears beneath our demands of what we declare to be the limits of his grace and love must be what a prophet sees. God knows a thing or two about suffering. He knows intimately about death. Incarnate, he came to grips with both. It behooves us to trust that his measure and value for suffering and death originate from an enlightened, heavenly position.

How else could he say we are blessed if we are persecuted like those who came before us, or blessed in the eyes of God is the death of his saints? Such an understanding comes only from clarity and focus gained through experiencing the Jesus field trips. Most of the time, I simply want less of the pain, less of the self-crucifixion, and less death in my dying to self.

Obviously I do not fully appreciate what I want. Knowing

Christ is too much knowledge. It is too much of God. He is love, but his love rips chaff off grain. The product is good, but the process incurs pain through tribulation.

Surprisingly, tribulation is a farming term, not a political or spiritual one. While conducting archaeological research on Roman-Byzantine farmsteads in the Hashemite Kingdom of Jordan, I came upon the root word "Tribulum." It describes a threshing sledge comprised of three (thus the tri), six to eight foot long, heavy, wooden beams, six inches thick by eight inches wide, the bottom sides of which were compactly studded with half-inch gravel about two inches apart. After the harvested grain has been thoroughly dried, the sheaves are placed atop the bedrock of the threshing floor, and the tribulum, pulled by an ox, is ridden over the grain, thoroughly threshing it.

The purpose of tribulation, then, is to produce chaff-free, life-giving, nourishing grain, a good thing.

It would appear from much of modern Christian literature concerning tribulation that its sole purpose is retribution, to punitively inflict pain and pulverize everything just for the sheer hell of it. Nothing could be further from the truth.

When pain, however, instructs our nomenclature of what is life, we miss an integral lesson. Pain is only a reminder that we are created for something vastly different. And no, pain is not joy. It is the deepest form of heartache at not being now what God originally created us to be. It is a constant thorn in the flesh to clarify our current situation and to focus us on who we are becoming.

God is no sadist. He knows there will soon be a time when tears and pain will cease. When pain becomes the point, we miss the point. We do not embrace personal pain, but neither do we drown it. Acknowledge pain's presence, mitigate against it, and do our level best to not add to it in ourselves or others. Given opportunities, we should alleviate pain whenever possible, because it is still an integral component of our fallenness.

As a certified nurse midwife, my wife reassures women in labor that within the context of childbirth, pain equals progress. She supports these women, to focus not on the pain, but on where this process is headed; new life within an overwhelming context of joy which supersedes the previous anguish. Like a midwife, Jesus does not belittle or negate our pain, he is simply trying to refocus us onto the joy set before us; new life, a new identity within an overwhelming context of glory.

LIKE A MIDWIFE, JESUS DOES NOT BELITTLE OR NEGATE OUR PAIN, HE IS SIMPLY TRYING TO REFOCUS US ONTO THE JOY SET BEFORE US: NEW LIFE, A NEW IDENTITY WITHIN AN OVERWHELMING CONTEXT OF GLORY.

Never is God more self-evident than at the end of suffering. Envision it: the wounded, bloodied corpse of his Holy Anointed, entombed, cold as the stone upon which it is laid. Place yourself there with the Disciples. Hear the cries of anguish. Embrace the despair, and bitter anger at being betrayed by what we see now were merely shallow, empty promises. Add to that the fear of being identified and taken as a follower of this dead, broken, seemingly false messiah.

Such was the Sad Sabbath following Good Friday. Sleepless, we pass the night rehashing our failures and igniting our fears.

But night deepens to its darkest right before daybreak, and the faint glimmer of light ascending in the east harbors no false hope or illusion. At life's darkest hour, God is kindling his dawn. At our lowest point of pain, God readies a resurrection to his highest heaven.

The question? God's purpose exceeds imagination.

The night? God's light is far too strong.

The corpse? His risen, eternal King of Glory.

Herein is victory. The nightmare is dispelled and the desperate, disquieting question of our "why" brilliantly resolves into the revelation of Emmanuel, our crucified, resurrected, ascended, with-us-through-exile God.

But does the pain not linger? Do the scars yet remain? Indeed they do, but not to remind us of past failure, but rather to further expound the immeasurable magnitude of his glory. For at the end of ALL suffering, in our new age-to-age species of time, grace still holds our hands to steady us in our lifting of our own eternal weight of God's Glory.

Psalm 46:1-3; 8-11 (KJV)

God is our refuge and strength,
a very present help in trouble.
Therefore will not we fear,
though the earth be removed,
and though the mountains be
carried into the midst of the sea;
Though the waters thereof roar
and be troubled, though the mountains shake
with the swelling thereof…
Come, behold the works of the LORD,
what desolations he hath made in the earth.
He maketh wars to cease
unto the end of the earth;
He breaketh the bow,
and cutteth the spear in sunder;
He burneth the chariot in the fire.
Be still, and know that I am God:
I will be exalted among the heathen,
I will be exalted in the earth.
The LORD of hosts is with us;
the God of Jacob is our refuge.

Chapter 5

Be Still, Be Amazed

In multiple ways, as a family, we have been abundantly blessed. But, as with all families, we harbor hidden, individual pains, secret sorrows that only hint at God's dealings with each of us. Among other griefs, our family carries the not-so-hidden, living grief of mental retardation—an adult-child. Of course, normally we use kinder, gentler terms like "cognitively delayed" or "special needs," words that feel softer and may make us feel better by masking our respective pain and loss.

Regardless of which words we use to define our daughter's condition, every missed milestone along life's road is a reminder of who and what she is not—that measure, of course, being calibrated by a cultural, physical, economic standard.

The birth of a child with disabilities feels like a barbed blessing that never blunts. Sometimes the full impact of that loss comes at us in ways least expected. Years have passed, and we feel this now to be an old, rheumatic-like pain. We have wept all the tears, drained dry the well of grief. Life goes on, the wound externally dressed. Then "Bam!" Out of nowhere—usually in times of great joy such as weddings, graduations, childbirth, life-defining events from which, experientially, she is excluded—sorrow floods the wellspring of that pain anew.

"Daddy, when we dance our father-daughter dance at my wedding . . ." I turn from her to quickly hide my grief. "Mommy, you will deliver my babies, won't you, Mommy?" Like Wordsworth, surprised by joy, tears, fresh, hot, humiliating, and raw issue forth as fountains of pain, loss, regret or fear. There is no balm in Gilead enough to soothe the heartbreak we thought we finally had reconciled. We lost everything in losing Eden.

My eyes have cried tears over the same loss decades apart, even knowing what I do of the temporality of pain. Even more than any fear of the unknown, it is the daily measure of her loss that continues to seep its pain, compounded by my inability, as her father, to fix it.

It is exactly who our daughter is that has allowed us, as a family, to intimately identify with the loss or pain of so many others around our world. God has redirected and focused our ways of seeing those whom our consumer-driven world call "the least of these."

Honestly, both our daughter and our family would prefer to have missed out on this pain, and the supposed lessons, in the same way we would jump out of the way of a careening bus. Sure, we have been consoled multiple times, by well-meaning people without disabled children, about "all God's lessons" we can learn from our daughter's disability. Of what value is my character or learned compassion compared to her disabilities? How can the two even be equated? How can I as her father ever be pleased about something I might gain at my child's expense?

I too at times have naively viewed another's suffering, disability, or loss as a divine instructional instrument or teachable moment to hopefully discover something deeper about who God is. But honestly, in what way would that be different than someone congratulating a couple on the birth of their child, stating what a blessing this is, as now, in the off chance the parents need, they could harvest a kidney or some other vital organ? As incomprehensible as that thought is, this is analogous to how the parent of a child with disabilities can feel in the face of such thoughtless, well-meaning platitudes.

I do not deny there are life lessons to learn. A child who touches a hot stove will not soon again touch even a cold one. God, however, is not the evangelist of ruin we so often portray him to be. He is not some capricious, cruel professor in the business of disabling, maiming, or killing people in order to teach some cosmic, beneficial, eternal lesson.

Christ came to die for our humanity. By turning our world right-side up, he disempowers and imprisons the invaders Sin and Death, redeeming us from the slavery and tyranny of their despotism. Now that is reckless love.

God owns the resounding victory. This is the Good News. Yes, turmoil still resides as a requisite component of our fallen, broken world, but not so God can teach us lessons. If there are indeed lessons still to be learned it is that God, being kind and compassionate, enters our catastrophes, redeems us, and salvages even our most tragic losses and the worst of our failings.

Through raising a child with special needs, we have discovered that God loves our daughter for who she is far more than he values any spiritual lessons or insights we might learn. Our daughter is a beautiful, loving, caring person, uniquely knit together from conception. Daily, our young family prayed for her during her gestation. She is God's adoring answer, barbs notwithstanding. We also love our daughter for who she is, regardless of what she has taught us about the nature or character of God.

God loves us, his whole humanity, in the same way. And yes, we are, to some measure, all spiritually retarded.

To illustrate such spiritual disability God provided an Old Testament story. It is a brilliant example of knowing only in part, seeing our world through an opaque glass, or corroded, tarnished bronze mirror.

Once there was a man named Gehazi. As the servant of Elisha, he was privileged to see things few others ever would, such as the raising of someone from the dead, the curing of leprosy, a floating, borrowed axehead. But the thing that should have most awakened his awareness to his spiritual disability was an incident in a remote town called Dothan in northern Samaria.

We read in II Kings 6 that an armed band of Aramaeans has surrounded Gehazi and Elisha by night. Check out this story. It actually reads like a spy novel. Elisha, being a prophet, is privy to every word spoken in the war counsel of the king of Damascus. So what does this Aramaean king do? He sends troops to capture and kill Elisha, like Elisha did not see that coming. Gehazi freaks out. "Oh, this is bad, this is really, really bad news."

Elisha scowls. "What are you talking about? There are more of us than them. And we have *them* surrounded." Elisha shakes his head. "Get a grip, noob!" Elisha points to the surrounding hills. Gehazi's eyes are opened to see those hills flanked with fiery troops alongside fiery horses hitched to fiery chariots.

One would think that having seen all these things Gehazi would be a champion of faith. But it is for good reason we do not name our children Gehazi. Remember that leprosy he saw cured? Naaman, a "nonbeliever," the commander of the same Aramaean army that tried to kill Elisha was the one who had it. God took it away. Want to talk about "love your enemies"? Gehazi, however, purchased that same leprosy with his guile and greed, for two bags of silver and two festal robes. That is spiritual disability.

Recognizing my own level of spiritual disability is helping me understand that at times, I too am tempted to fabricate a diminutive god reflexive of my spiritual impairments. More tragic still is our fictionalization of a god based upon our political and cultural Christianity. Such petty divinities cannot even approximate who God wishes to reveal himself to be through our waiting on him for answers, and being still within no answer.

I have not seen the hills around me studded with fiery angels. I have not witnessed the raising of the dead. I have not been provided an answer as to the suffering incumbent in children with disabilities. Through solitude and silence, however, I am learning to believe God knows what he's about. Through decades of Jesus field trips, God continues to draw me into relationship nurturing a humble, genuine, childlike heart, keenly aware of my spiritual disability.

RECOGNIZING MY OWN LEVEL OF SPIRITUAL DISABILITY IS HELPING ME UNDERSTAND THAT AT TIMES, I TOO AM TEMPTED TO FABRICATE A DIMINUTIVE GOD REFLEXIVE OF MY SPIRITUAL IMPAIRMENTS. MORE TRAGIC STILL IS OUR FICTIONALIZATION OF A GOD BASED UPON OUR POLITICAL AND CULTURAL CHRISTIANITY.

God accomplishes this impossible task, stripping us through our being poured out in out-of-the-way places. It is here where the hardest work for a Christian who puts hand to plow is being still to know God is God and we are not.

Prior to starting college, I participated in a ten-day climbing, hiking trip into the backcountry of the high Sierra Nevadas, a field trip of sorts. This class was designed to impart two things: work interdependently with the seven others as a team, and learn solitude. The second was by far the more difficult.

For twenty-four hours, alone, remote on the steep side of a mountain slope called the Sawtooth Ridge, I sat buttressed against a granite facing, uttering not a word, trying to absorb the grandeur that was God. No food, no water, no sleeping bag, nothing but me. What an astonishing, agonizing, beautiful, awe-filled experience to observe and reflect that in the enormity of God's universe, looking up into the immensity of the meteoric-strewn Milky Way, God knew me and loved me and *he* was going to walk me back into his eternal heaven. Solitude has its blessings.

There are elements to learning more of God—vital, integral elements such as gentleness and humility—that can only be experienced in the solitude of waiting and being still.

On our wilderness excursion, we were told, there is one fundamental rule if you get lost. "Stay where you are. We will come to find you." As exiles out of Eden, this is God's rule as well. He knows we are lost. "Be still. Know I am God. I am on my way to rescue you."

The shared spiritual landscape of our pilgrimage, our wilderness wanderings, is similar to another's only in the most rudimentary of ways. Each person's path up the mountains of faith, or through the deserts of spiritual abuse, our own Jesus field trips, traverse by ways none have trod before. As each day is unique, so each place in each day has its own joys and discoveries, trials and triumphs.

But the need for solitude is universal. The need to stop and reflect is essential to regain our bearings, to evaluate where we have been and where from here the road may next lead. Being spiritually disabled, we need to wait for God to come alongside us, to rescue us. We are lost. God is on his way to find us.

Sadly, in seeking after God, some of us keep a frenetic pace so as to avoid delays. We soon find ourselves doubly lost. The more we quicken our steps the more lost we become. Only small, fragile, simplistic Sunday-school answers and discord accompany the clamoring throng of such a congregation. We join company and continue to encourage the tempo, all the while offering platitudes and congratulations for being "a faithful believer" and keeping to the "right" path.

Being still, waiting upon God, the quiet heart knows deep, desolate truth and, yes, loneliness.

The frantic heart knows nothing; it simply emotes, shrieking to stop the deafening noise of its own cognitive dissonance. By the end of such a spiritual journey there is a heightened lunacy and a tendency towards legalistic cannibalism. *"Be still? Are you kidding; not if my life depended upon it!"*

But such spiritual disability is never what God intended.
Tragically, so much of what we have been taught about who

God is has been imbued with our cultures, our economies, and our politics, all of which are read and interpreted through our limited, boxed-in, upside down, opaque-windowed personal experiences and private pain. And thus, when God approaches our lost humanity with a heart of compassion for the suffering—the poor, the refugee, the "sinner"—we ply simple answers, we blame the victims, we take comfort in our myopic, spiritually disabled view of rightness.

By failing to fully embrace God's call for compassion, we in essence, like Pilate and the Pharisees, scourge God with our doctrines, curse him through our dogmas, and crucify him within our petty theologies. And we think, through it all, that we have done well, that somehow we have instructed God to be God.

Be still! Our life does depend on it.

In Matthew's first recorded teachings of Jesus, chapters five through seven, in what we now call the Sermon on the Mount, he sets out the parameters of what a Kingdom one would look like. In essence, Jesus says in Matthew 7:21-23, "Don't pretend to know me. Relationship matters."

For any number of reasons, many assert the title, "Select of God." Some even go so far as to claim proprietorship over righteousness doing in his name. "Lord, Lord, did I not set people straight as to what to believe about you? Did I not safeguard heaven's gates? I even built an empire upon the promises of miracles, the promises of salvation. Look at me, look at meeee. Tell me I'm pretty."

Unimpressed Jesus turns and states, "Who in hell are you?"

In Matthew's very last recorded teaching of Jesus, chapter 25, we have a similar theme. Sitting upon his throne, Jesus invites the gentle ones in. "Enter into the kingdom, most-beloved. In feeding the poor, you fed me. You provided water to the filthy and thirsty. I desperately needed that. You didn't call me an illegal alien, a foreigner, or a worthless bum. Seeing beyond skin color, you called me brother. You clothed me and cared for me, naked and diseased as I was. And in prison, you saw my humanity, my in-between state of who I had been and who, through grace, God was making me to be. All you did or neglected to do for the least of these, my siblings, you have done, or not done unto me."

Relationship is not what we claim to know about God, it is what God says and knows of us. In relationship, he knows us either as his children or not. We do not make that judgment. In solitude we learn that God longs for right relationship, not simply correct doctrine. There is a world of difference between knowing God intimately, experientially, loving and relating to him vs. simply intellectually, accumulating fact sheets about him.

God does desire us to know him. He has always kept the communication channels open so he might speak his word into our hearts. He even went so far as to become the Word incarnate in order to end silence as we have come to know it.

We should approach God in serene silence, for anything we attempt to add is noise. Our monkey chatter is supremely out of place in the corridors of heaven. We need to open our eyes and ears, walk tall, and learn of him. But how? *"Be still—and know—that I am God!"*

IN SOLITUDE WE LEARN THAT GOD LONGS FOR RIGHT RELATIONSHIP, NOT SIMPLY CORRECT DOCTRINE. THERE IS A WORLD OF DIFFERENCE.

Be amazed and happily embrace the humility of having to recognize that simple truth again. God comes riding on the clouds, fire in his eyes, but also a twinkle, because he is looking at us. A smile crosses his lips as he speaks, "My child, what joy did you find in me today?"

Be still. Be amazed. Know he is God.

God Knows What He's About

When God wants to drill a man
And thrill a man and skill a man,
When God wants to mold a man
To play the noblest part;
When He yearns with all His heart
To create so great and bold a man
That all the world shall be amazed,
Watch His methods, watch his ways!
How He ruthlessly perfects
Whom He royally elects!
How He hammers him and hurts him,
And with mighty blows converts him
Into trial shapes of clay which
Only God understands;
While his tortured heart is crying
And he lifts beseeching hands!
How He bends but never breaks
When his good God undertakes;
How He uses whom He chooses
And with every purpose fuses him;
By every act induces Him
To try his splendor out—
God knows what He's about!

Unknown

Chapter 6

Of Value and Nothing

Being poured out as an offering unto God seems the end of that which is poured out. But only flesh tells us thus. For when God receives an offering, like the barley loaves and fish fingerlings, it is multiplied thousands-fold. And its benefit honors and glorifies his name. This defines the life of living the daily sacrifice, of taking up our cross, of being poured out unto God.

But with careful words and reason we will be told to be wise stewards. God must truly not desire that we would sell all we have and give it to the poor. That was only for one man. Perhaps.

From dealings with other rich, young power-brokers and what I have come to understand of the cultural contexts of Jesus' day, I am convinced it is not the rich, young ruler's wealth that turns his heart from God. He wants to serve God, which is why he asked the question in the first place. It's simply that his wealth has become the only means by which he feels he can secure God's favor. More than likely, it is his religiosity of righteousness doing which prevents his heart from being turned from his wealth. Within his search for significance, tied to a cultural understanding of God, he brings his shiny pebbles and broken shell bits before God's throne. This poor man wrongly imagines God desires or values such debris in the same measure as does the rest of the world.

God desires our hearts, not our wealth. I find it hard to imagine that the God who, with a word, created all the gold and diamonds that ever existed, would want or need our money. He asks that we relinquish our wealth for our spiritual, eternal gain, not his. God may use wealth to build community, to teach us spiritual discipline, to allow us to participate in his kingdom. But, he does not need our money. Our material assets are valueless to him. He knows that only our empty hands have the freedom to grasp true and eternal treasure. How simpleminded we become when we reduce God's economy to gold and doing, forgetting that the currency of heaven is blood and grace.

When we give up what counts for nothing, God's "goodies", to claim what his heart is all about, the goodness of God, only then, with God's eye on the widow's mite, can we relinquish all that defines us. For only then can we understand that material wealth is placed in the negative column of God's ledger.

HOW SIMPLEMINDED WE BECOME WHEN WE REDUCE GOD'S ECONOMY TO GOLD AND DOING, FORGETTING THAT THE CURRENCY OF HEAVEN IS BLOOD AND GRACE.

At times, God has taken his most profitable servants out

of commission for various periods of their lives, and they undoubtedly chafed at the bit. Such an investment would, to us, measure as a waste of time and good talent. But God's ways are not our ways, because he will not share his glory with another. God is not careful or calculating with his resources, or so it would seem.

Too often God squanders truly brilliant men and women, sending them off to obscure places to do even more obscure things. Or he allows limited resources to be consumed for the petty passions of the flesh and the pride of life.

Moses, the former prince of Egypt, shepherded for forty years in Sinai, learning to not speak. Elijah sat quietly near a small river-bed in Jordan for three years, and only learned obedience. Isaiah and Jeremiah spent their most productive years preaching to people whose ears and hearts had been closed by the same God who had sent them. Paul stayed fourteen years in Arabia learning not only what he would suffer for the sake of the cross, but how to embrace the grace to endure it.

"His eye is on the sparrow and I know he watches me."

God never wastes time. He may squander everything else, but he never wastes time. And once we have been silenced and hid by God, then we learn that God knows what he is about. And then we learn that he never wastes anything. Indeed, he is lavish with his resources, and he makes each raindrop accomplish its errand.

Speaking of rain, I have something I need to confess. At one time I was that self-assured minister up in the pulpit thinking I had God all figured out. I felt it my duty to give out my answers as if they were God's. I thought I genuinely loved people, but God was about to teach me a harsh, valuable lesson, by letting me see inside my true heart.

Our small family traveled the treacherous, mountain road down to a small mission hospital in the southern region of Yemen to be with friends, some of whom a decade later would be martyred. For two years now, drought had lingered. As we drove through town, we noticed uncharacteristically large crowds milling about the dusty street and open market space. Upon inquiring, we were excitedly told that the local Imam, the religious leader, had gathered the community to pray for rain. They had gone to the top of the adjacent hill and slaughtered two cows as an offering, a petition to God. *How quaint.*

I drove on up to the mission guest house, whipped out my Bible and started to read the Elijah on Mt. Carmel story, planning the next morning to venture to the top of that blood-covered hill and pray loud and long for rain to prove that my God, he's the true God.

Presently though, I was disturbed from my holy hubris, my pompous reading, and small-minded plotting by the sound of distant, rolling thunder. I strode out of the small house just in time to see dark, billowing clouds come roiling across the mountain tops. Flashes of lightning followed by bellowing thunder shook every corner of that drought-stricken land. And then drops, sloppy and plump, plopped and plinked their way onto my angry face, as God graciously answered those desperate people's heart-felt prayers.

He loved on those people in terms they understood. Those two cows must have been something special, because for three whole days and nights it rained. And I, silent and sullen like Jonah, chafed at a God who would take away *my* victory by answering a day too soon.

Shriveled was my heart. Barren was my soul. So small had become this God my cultural Christianity had manufactured, this God who only selectively saves, loves, and blesses. I scoured scripture trying to salvage what little I could of the faith I still held in this fickle deity. But in the end, God's answer was for him to be far bigger than I had wanted him to be.

He had brought me to Yemen, not so I could save the "Lost," but so he could rescue me from everything I had ever been or hoped to be. From that moment he started to strip me of the fragile identity I had safeguarded in my belief in a diminutive divinity. He began to divest me of my cultural Christianity. He began to break open this small heart in which I had held even smaller idols.

God *loves* people. How could I have missed that in Jesus? I, for one, had not always "been saved." While I, a lost sinner, was shaking my fist in God's face, Christ died for me. He did not wait to love me, hoping I would get my act together. As we are told in Romans 5:8 JB,

"But what proves that God loves us is that Christ died for us while we were still sinners."

In the same way, that blood-covered hill in Yemen was counted as faith in another blood-covered hill just north of Jerusalem, even if they didn't know it in the exact way I did.

God was doing the saving. I was arrogantly standing in his way. From that point on, I have attempted simply to love people. I began to see folks as God views us all: works-of-grace-in-process in his capable hands.

Somewhere along the line I had ascribed to the belief that "unbelievers" were peons in some cosmic Amway deal wherein the more people I converted or "saved" the greater my reward in heaven. I loved God, I truly did. I had dedicated my whole life and that of my family to him.

There is a simple truth with God: he will not share his glory with another. He will wait for as long as it takes, to hide us away and pour us out if necessary, to ensure we are pure vessels to carry grace. There has been a tremendous amount of stripping of self since that mountain-top encounter. And it continues still. The Jesus field trips provide lessons in the out-of-the-way places God takes us in order to prepare us to glimpse the bigger heart God has for all people.

IN THE END, GOD'S ANSWER WAS FOR HIM TO BE FAR BIGGER THAN I HAD WANTED HIM TO BE.

As he did for the Disciples, so he will do for us. The Disciples changed the world, because they finally, unfettered by their religious demands and cultural expectations of Christ, owned the good news that God loves people. And that is one of the greatest blessings a shriveled, petty, self-focused heart can ever hope to learn.

Thou Art Indeed Just, Lord

Justus quidem tu es, Domine, si disputem tecum;
verumtamen justa loquar ad te:
Quare via impiorum prosperatur?

Jeremiah 12:1

Thou art indeed just, Lord, if I contend
With thee; but, sir, so what I plead is just.
Why do sinners' ways prosper? and why must
Disappointment all I endeavour end?

Wert thou my enemy, O thou my friend,
How wouldst thou worse, I wonder, than thou dost
Defeat, thwart me? Oh, the sots and thralls of lust
Do in spare hours more thrive than I that spend,

Sir, life upon thy cause. See, banks and brakes
Now leavèd how thick! lacèd they are again
With fretty chervil, look, and fresh wind shakes

Them; birds build -- but not I build; no, but strain,
Time's eunuch, and not breed one work that wakes.
Mine, O thou lord of life, send my roots rain.

Gerard Manley Hopkins

Chapter 7

Unfettered Mystery

Water is wet. The sky is blue. Infiniteness is unquantifiable. Sometimes, because a fact seems common or patently obvious we fail to grasp how simply profound is its truth. Everything that defines us within our corporeal nature is itself a boundary. The corollary is that since God is boundless, immaterial, supra-substantive, no human definition suffices. Divinity constitutes a condition our physicality could never fathom.

To declare that God is omnipotent is not entirely true. He surpasses omnipotence. He is not simply all powerful; he transcends even our feeble, fractured notion of what establishes power. Regardless of any language with which to express given ideas about God, the words and ideas are themselves gravely inadequate to comprehend, let alone define, the Divine.

Any given thing, irrespective of my ability to describe it, is itself its own definition. The child sees a flower and declares it beautiful. A botanist lists its classification and physiology. Neither sees more accurately—only differently. And yet, had the flower never been perceived, hidden in some alpine meadow, it would still exist in its full complexity and beauty. It would still sing its full glory to its Creator.

Perceptions, our very pathways of knowing have been taught. I was born on the border of the Tarzan-like jungles of Congo's Ituri rainforest; an unbroken swath of giant mahogany methuselahs shouldering a burden of vegetative anarchy in riot. Millions of acres in area, it offers no horizon. There, the farthest distance is a Pigmy bow-shot.

The Forest-people, as they call themselves, wondered then, at the magic that allowed a flying thing, no bigger than a man's thumb, to grow into the giant metal machine that could hold bananas, boxes, barrels and people. Lacking a concept of depth perception, they literally could not comprehend that an object farther away only looked small.

Once, one of these Forest-people was flying between stations with my dad, and he saw in a clearing below a herd of elephants. Upon inquiry, he was incredulous. "Where I come from, elephants are very big. Yours are no bigger than ants!" To his mind, only magic provided an answer.

Back in our world, every word carries its own history, its own burden of bias. What I claim to know is merely a construct of my own personal experiences, a product of my individual, finite, empirical frame of reference. The world in which I function exists to me only in so far as I can engage and relate to it.

Imagine a young woman standing on the street corner in some university town, cardboard sign advertising her plight. A BMW pulls up, a student late for class. The woman on the street and the student share the same physical space, but little else of this world. For the student, the buildings on campus represent a future, access to power, money, prestige. To the other young lady, these represent a barrier, a denial of power, money and prestige.

Much of the distinction between these two was made through the choices of others. Their respective mental constructs now determine not only how they paint their world, but any additional future choices they can or will make.

The physicality of our world is not accessed in the same way by each person. There is a mental landscape that informs how I view the actual landscape. I become an artist, capturing not what is, but only how I perceive. I am a photographer not simply of light but across time and space. Since I was a child, how I have perceived and related to my world has shifted. Over time, new experiences, education, opportunities, and relationships inform my ways of knowing, radically shifting not only what, but how I perceive.

Everything I claim as intellect or seek as knowledge subsists only as a prejudice, a pre-positioning toward a particular way of knowing, an approximation drawn upon my smudged slate of awareness. As patently obvious as the old cliché, the mind *can* know only its own thoughts.

The same then is true of my greater task of seeking, in faith, to know God. The child or theologian sees only what each has been taught to observe. Neither sees more accurately than the other, each simply sees differently.

When the theologian propounds great thoughts about God, he says the same thing as does the child; the only difference is the jargon, the technical terminology and the use of lots of big words. Both are woefully insufficient to describe the infinite, our Love Divine. All of humanity's knowledge adds nothing to God's true, infinite definition, for one cannot add to infinity.

God is God. There is no "And." What we perceive God to be, as St. Paul reminds us, is a poor, grimy reflection. To be clear, the limitation of our humanity is not inherently a problem for God. God is big enough to reach across our inability, into our frailty and reveal his saving word. Our seeking to know and live in relationship with him is simply our response to his first seeking us, his knowing us, his saving us.

Remember Jesus' teaching on the final judgment in Matthew? Nothing we claim to have known or done for God produces salvation, but rather God knowing us. Seeking, therefore, on our part demands humility—an accurate assessment of ourselves in light of who God is; grace—an acceptance of God's sufficiency without merit; and faith— believing God knows what he's about despite the periods of silence.

THE LIMITATION OF OUR HUMANITY IS NOT INHERENTLY A PROBLEM FOR GOD. GOD IS BIG ENOUGH TO REACH ACROSS OUR INABILITY, INTO OUR FRAILTY AND REVEAL HIS SAVING WORD.

Problems arise when we employ a self-standard as our measure by which we say we know God. By fabricating an anthropocentric theology, we confuse a mere reflection with being the source of light itself.

Even a full moon cannot blind, but look too long at the sun and that will be the last you see. God, as Sun, will not only blind us, he will consume us. As we read in the last verse of Hebrews 12, our God is a consuming fire, and his fire both devours and refines.

When Satan made a Mephistophelian bargain with God over the person of Job, Job suffered. And he also worshiped. And then through thirty-five chapters of philosophizing God offers no clue as to his purposes for Job's sufferings.

Job never knew the backstory. Faith is all Job is left with after the blather and "comfort" of his friends.

Then God speaks for five more chapters, expounding upon his own greatness and majesty. He starts with,

"Who is this obscuring my designs with his empty-headed words?"

He continues,

"Who laid (Earth's) cornerstone when all the stars of the morning were singing with joy, and the Sons of God in chorus were chanting praise?"

Job 38:2, 6-7 JB

Job's humble response is telling.

"I was the man who misrepresented your intentions with my ignorant words. Before, I knew you only by hearsay, but now, having seen you with my own eyes, I retract what I have said, and repent in dust and ashes."

Job 42:3, 5-6 NJB

God ends his monotribe by saying to Eliphaz,
"I burn with anger against you and your two friends for not speaking truthfully about me as my servant Job has done."

Job 42:7 NJB

Whereas Job continues to worship in faith despite the pain, the loss, and yes, even the silence, Eliphaz and comrades, like Spafford's church, fearful of a god too big and incapacitated by the "problem of pain," point the finger. How rarely we preach on that last verse from Job. That sermon might clear the pews.

It kind of makes one wonder how God feels about those loudly claiming Christ while carrying placards, proclaiming "God Hates Fags." Everything in the Gospels leads me to believe this upside down reflection is not only distorted, it is actually a 180 degrees reversal. In contradistinction, the Gospels clearly reveal a Jesus showering his love upon prostitutes, Samaritans, pagan demoniacs, a disciple named Judas.

In John eight we are told of an adulterous woman dragged before Jesus by the respectable right, the teachers of law,

74

and the angry guardians of Heaven's gates. There, they demand of him a verdict. Jesus bends down and on the ground writes with his finger. I doubt he draws stick figures. He probably writes, "Gossip, Malice, Bitterness, Avarice, Discord, Slander, Grasping, Self-righteousness, Arrogance." He stands, "I could go on." That vengeful, hate-filled mob slowly dissipates back into their diminished sense of self-righteous, religious propriety. Jesus turns to the woman. "And your accusers?"

"There are . . . none, Sir." Her eyes hold a fragile measure of hope and an abundance of fear.

With his foot, Jesus erases the sins inscribed in the dust and smiles. "Then neither do I condemn. I set you free to sin no more."

When we do preach on Job, we skim over the verses condemning the self-important yammering of Job's friends, and God's evident anger at being misrepresented. We instead prefer to focus on the fact that Job was re-blessed with double of everything, including beautiful daughters. Isn't it nice how everything works out well in the end?

Lest we forget, Job's first children and his first servants, like the Spafford children, never saw that "happy ever after." There were no cosmic, eternal lessons for them to learn. The only way I might comprehend such casualties of God's sovereignty is to be still, to walk by faith, not by sight, even in the sorrow, even in the silence of knowing that he alone is God. He alone knows what he's about.

Mystery does indeed present problems for us. We are

uncomfortable with unanswerable questions. We feel ill-equipped for faith in an unfathomable God. We thus weave our own backstory, our own theory of what God is about.

Like Job's friends, thinking we are doing Jesus a favor by defending his honor, we too freely provide blather, a false narrative, and an accusatory finger.

Our lack of faith, grounded in our lack of humility, results in our lack of empathy or grace toward those being shaped like clay in the Potter's hands, or toward those who endure as collateral damage of having been born into a fallen, broken world. We prefer to find fault, to chide God's children for their suffering.

THE GOSPELS CLEARLY REVEAL A JESUS SHOWERING HIS LOVE UPON PROSTITUTES, SAMARITANS, PAGAN DEMONIACS, A DISCIPLE NAMED JUDAS.

Speaking of clay, in John nine we hear the Disciples, coming upon a man born blind and asking within earshot of the man, "Whose sin did this?"

Jesus gives a furrowed-brow. "Whaaaat? Sin? Is that how you see me?" He walks over to the man and lifting him by the hand states, "This man represents glory in a long-time-coming kind of way. His loss has been a difficult grace, a severe kind of mercy." Jesus then makes clay, builds a set of new eyes for the man and sends him off to wash away his blindness.

But Jesus doesn't stop there. In Luke seven he allows a

prostitute to wash his feet with her tears and dry them with her hair. In traditional Middle Eastern contexts, women's hair must always be covered. There is even a saying that an angel, a messenger of God, will never visit a house where the rafters have seen the bare head of a woman.

Like the Pharisees, we too are scandalized when, instead of righteous condemnation, he offers grace. "Leave her alone." Jesus scorns our offence. "What she has done is beautiful worship." He then turns to the woman. "I love what you've done with your hair." He smiles at the Pharisee's scowl. Returning his attention to the woman he states as a tear of joy crests it banks, "Woman, your multitude of sins are forgiven. Your faith is rewarded. Saved now, go your way in peace."

Often, however, we still chastise Jesus, accusing him of being a love-drunk, grace-giving profligate. "Look, he's a friend of . . . (righteous gasp and indignation, then pause for emphasis) . . . Sinners!" By preferring to blame the victims, instead of lending a hand, we throw stones. Jesus' eyes blaze, burning with anger for not speaking gospel truth. You want to talk "sinners in the hands of an angry God"?

We are left with two options, two standpoints or frameworks from which to proclaim God's good news. We can be as Job, a man quietly trusting God's heart through the suffering, through the silence, through the embarrassed, self-righteous condemnations of our friends. Or, we can be Job's friends, defending God's honor by blaspheming him, chastising his Anointed, and slamming the very sinners he came to love back into salvation.

Like Job, in faith, we know God is not silent in his silence. The stars still sing; the Children of God still praise. God is singing to himself a song of victory and triumph. He is orchestrating his magnum opus. The universe pulses with his vibrato.

God is there. And his eyes moisten with joy and pride when he sees each of us struggle amidst the mystery, like Job or Spafford, living as if we can hear the symphony, living, knowing he does love and care for us even in the haunting of no answer.

The "silence field trip" is one of the most difficult. But this field trip is designed to strip us of our assuredness that we have figured God out. It is God, not our understanding of him that guarantees hope.

Together, the congregation of former sinners listens to the lyric of Heaven's anthem. The Curse is lifted,

"His servants will worship him, they will see him face to face, and his name will be written on their foreheads. It will never be night again and they will not need lamplight or sunlight, because the Lord God will be shining on them. They will reign for ever and ever."

Revelation 22:3-5 JB

Then, through his grace, all silence will cease. Always.

Job 19:24-27 JB

"This I know: that my Avenger lives, and he, the Last, will take his stand on earth. After my awaking, he will set me close to him, and from my flesh, I shall look on God. He whom I shall see will take my part: these eyes will gaze on him and find him not aloof."

Chapter 8

Childlike Greatness

As children, recipients and conduits of God's grace, we are commissioned to proclaim the good news of God's completed, sacrificial provision for our world. God's grace functions within a radical inclusivity. Boldly, as he did on the cross, he declares that we too are to love our enemies and pray for those who persecute us (Matthew 5:44). He is not asking us to change people, or judge them, or condemn them, or picket them, or kill them. Pray and Love. Pretty basic.

But even the disciples had difficulty with this field trip. Short-term missions, to places far-afield, has its place in maturing our faith. But these should be designed as a primer, a field trip to learn what God's about. Often, however, short-term missions never rises above the level of a compassion holiday or tragedy tourism. Those are not our poor, our sick, our lost. Afterward, feeling significant and fulfilled, we get to return to our normal, unaltered lives. Loving people closer to home, that's a truer, often more difficult calling. At home I am forced to accommodate or vary routines. Discipleship will cost me an ongoing investment of myself, my time, and emotions without an exit strategy.

In Matthew 19 we are told that some folks, undoubtedly less-educated, welfare types, bad teeth, body odor, on Obamacare, brought little children to Jesus for him to pray a blessing on them. The disciples shooed them away.

Having lived in the Middle East and Africa most of my life, and therefore, having interacted with my share of people living without indoor plumbing, I can sympathize with the disciples on this one. "Snotty little, disease-ridden street urchins. Judas, keep an eye on that money bag."

Jesus, an eyebrow raised, states, "Seriously?" He points to the retreating, rejected mob. "These guys *own* the Kingdom." Having called the kids back, he sits down on a clump of grass. He pulls a silver denarii out of a little girl's ear, then plops it in her filthy hand, and whispers. "Take it. Money is valueless where I come from." Shocked, Judas clutches the money bag. Jesus kisses the forehead of a kid with mange and winks. "I like what you've done to your hair." Another kid, head roiling with lice, snuggles close. Jesus musses up his already disheveled hair, and grins from ear to ear. Turning to the disciples he yells, "Group hug!"

Grown men, Jesus' disciples, look on with fear and disgust. Jesus laughs, "The Kingdom belongs to such as these. Get with the program. Embrace the gospel truth."

This is the God I believe in. What I do not believe in is

the complicit, capricious deity invoked by many of today's politicos or by the culturally expedient church. True good news as Jesus lives out in the Gospels, is radically at odds with that image of a divisive deity who plays favorites, takes sides in war, or salivates for damnation and end times. That is not the God revealed in Jesus.

Having tabernacled among us, Jesus no longer is marred by our supposed sins done against him. He's already dealt with humanity's sin fully on a cross, sealed it within a tomb, and by means of his resurrection, utterly and irrevocably removed its stain. We cannot now add a sin to the cross that he has not already covered. Our love can create a refuge from life's fallenness and a path into grace that our condemnation never will. That's excellent news.

Reflectively, we need to view our upside downness for what it is, dis-equilibrating. We can begin to bask anew in the glory of who God has made each of us, his dearly beloved child.

In God's ever expansive Heaven, I am told, dwell three types of people: those I expect to see, those I do not expect to see, and those who do not expect to see me. God alone knows his own. It is he alone who calls each of us by name, according to *his* purpose and according to *his* glory. His love seeks us out. His love finds us.

In God there exists no hint of nepotism, no predestination of his little darlings and his unselect, horrid little damned. No "saved" and "them others." In Christ, there are no second-class citizens, no classification of illegal-alien or minority.

Colossians 3:11 declares that our new self, our icon continually being renewed in the image of our Creator, provides no room for distinction between 'Greek and Jew, circumcised and uncircumcised, barbarian, Scythian (basically outlaw cowboys more barbarous than barbarians), free and slave.' In Christ, there exists a unity not only of purpose, but of being.

Every person will stand naked before Christ carrying only his or her measure of faith and obedience. Scripture clearly states, every knee will bow before the throne of grace, and every tongue confess fealty to the King crowned in thorns. Scripture does not say that I get to determine when or how that comes about.

OUR LOVE CAN CREATE A REFUGE FROM LIFE'S FALLENNESS AND A PATH INTO GRACE THAT OUR CONDEMNATION NEVER WILL.

In Matthew nine we read the account of Jesus' call of Matthew. This disciple introduces his self-story, proudly declaring that at the celebration table that night were some of his close friends, "sinners and tax collectors!" Read here, "whores, swindlers, profligates, tattooed floozies, gays and Roman collaborators." Oh MY!

In response to the Pharisees' disdain Jesus responds, "The healthy don't seek a doctor, but the sick do. That's why I have come." Jesus smiles and sweeps his hand across the crowded room. "The doctor is in the house."

"Hazaaaah!" cheers the crowd.

Jesus, wine goblet raised, smiles. "Read Hosea, the prophet

commanded to marry a hooker. So what do you think it means when it says,

"Faithful love is what pleases me, not sacrifice; knowledge of God, not burnt offerings."

Right relationship over "right doctrine." Of what value is our fighting the culture wars compared to living within the efficacy of grace? It is the efficacious shed blood of Jesus that saves us, not some presumed pedigree or recitation of a simplistic sinner's prayer. Salvation is by no means a foregone conclusion. It is a to-be promise, and all of that is God's doing, none of ours.

A few months after Matthew's get-to-know-Jesus mixer, actually the night following Jesus' cleansing the temple of religiously sanctified extortion, *the* Teacher of Israel comes to Jesus under cover of dark in order to instruct this little Galilean upstart on a few rules regarding temple etiquette.

Within the Rabbinical tradition of instruction, in order to carefully frame the parameters of an argument or set forth the points of a discussion, one normally opened with a question. Remember, the religious leaders of the day were inimically concerned with law. They loved to be seen in public and to put people in their place.These were religious lawyers. The minutia of law genuinely mattered to them.

Consider then how many times Jesus, in confronting their hypocrisy, either starts with or answers with a question.

"Is it permitted on the Sabbath day to do good, or to do evil?"

Mark 3:4 NJB

"Have you not read this text in Scripture: The stone which the builders rejected has become the cornerstone?"

Mark 12:10 NJB

"Why do you break away from the commandments of God for the sake of your traditions?"

Matthew 15: 3 NJB

"What can anyone offer in exchange for his life?"

Matthew 16:26 NJB

So in John 3 when we find Nicodemus coming privately at night, starting without a question, our eyebrows should be raised. This meeting is not intended to be an inquiry. It is premeditated to be an inquisition.

Lest we forget, there were no chapter breaks in the original narrative. The end of chapter two of John is the prelude to the Nicodemus story.

"Jesus knew all people and he did not trust himself to

them; he never needed evidence about anyone; he could tell what someone had in him."

John 2:24-25 NJB

Enter then, Nicodemus with his dossier on Jesus in hand. "We know who you are," (cough), *or rather who you think you are.* (Smile, blink rapidly.) *"We respect that you are a teacher . . . er . . . from God riiiight . . ."*

Jesus holds up a finger. "Hear some Truth with a capital "T." No one can see God's Kingdom unless first born spiritually, from above. Don't come here trying to teach me the rules of the game when you don't even know what game we're supposed to be playing."

Nicodemus, put out at having been both interrupted and scolded, nearly jumps out of his chair. "Look here, little whippersnapper, what you're suggesting is downright obscene. Born again? What nonsense. Return to my mother's womb? Pervert!"

That conversation did not end there. We know that Nicodemus did eventually understand. He did, like a little child, having been born from above, fully embrace the kingdom. And later still, boldly living out the gospel, he stood before Pilate, shoulder to shoulder with Joseph of Arimathaea, asking for the body of his slain, brutalized, "righteously rejected" messiah. Nicodemus, the top religious scholar of his day, understood that Jesus had indeed come, *"not to judge the world, but so that through him (this sacrificial death), the world might be saved."* (John 3:17 NJB) Such is the power of Good News.

Jesus redefines our upside-down world. Victory is a cross, self-death is true life, love for our enemies brings wholeness to humanity, his peace brings a sword, the meek inherit the earth, the last come first, and childlike faith ushers us into heaven. As Nicodemus had to learn, this is exactly opposite from our cultural, political churchianity.

I began to learn this for myself while in Yemen where our next door neighbor was the chief Imam, the top religious leader for the entire country. He was a good man, a gracious man, a godly man. On the walls of his house, in English and Arabic, were framed quotes from the Bible given to him and his wife by their Christian Filipina housekeeper.

"The sheep that belong to me listen to my voice; I know them and they follow me. I give them eternal life."
John 10:27-28a JB

In the three years we lived as neighbors, it increasingly became evident this man lived gospel, exhibiting more Christ-likeness than pretty much anyone else I met, Christian or Muslim. Exemplary of his character, his wife of many decades remained barren, but he refused to marry another in contradistinction to all cultural and religious expectation. He chose the way of Jesus instead.

God chose a Filipina housekeeper to influence Yemen in ways my education, my titles, my theology, and my passport never could. God's call. God's purpose. God's minister. All for God's glory.

This story is replicated multifold across the Middle East and elsewhere. Christians: nurses from India, house servants from the Philippines, African brothers and sisters from across that continent, working in near slave-like conditions, spreading the Gospel, humbly, joyfully, boldly, in pure, childlike faith. Like Jesus, living gospel in word and deed, they love people.

Christianity is not merely an inventory of doctrines to believe, not simply a creed or set of moralistic codes. Faith is a relationship, an abiding with Christ, the living eternal, incarnate God. Likewise, missions cannot simply remain a project or a canned message we preach. Discipleship is incarnational, the lived-out expression of authentic relationship with people in the world around us. This Good News changes people.

The Franciscans and other Catholic communities of faith have a long, beautiful tradition of sent-ones. Not so long ago, Protestant missionaries were living the same way. In the late 1880's, those called to Africa packed their few belongings in coffins knowing they would never return to what they had once called home. Nearly two centuries before, the Moravians, in what is now the Czech Republic, the first protestant church, sent missionaries around the world through a simple devotion to loving Christ.

Once commissioned, usually in twos or threes, these missionaries were given enough to travel to the nearest port. From there they were required to work for passage across whichever ocean took them to their calling. Having arrived, they took up whatever occupation would provide a minimal amount to be fed and clothed, and there lived out the gospel.

In Barbados, they became the first church to include slaves in their congregation. Some Moravians even sold themselves as indentured servants in order to reach slave communities in the Caribbean. When it came to standing for justice, they were the only church that walked the Trail of Tears with our Cherokee, brothers and sisters. Living Christ's gospel changes people.

I fear we have lost sight of the fact that greatness is not the same as notoriety. The titles we crave in our Christianity, the nomenclature we claim as our exclusive domain, add nothing to what God has already declared concerning who we are. Our mission budgets or outreach programs are, more often than not, measured by numbers of people sent and dollars spent rather than in grace given or mercy received. There is only an audience of One, and it is his opinion and knowledge of us that ultimately matters.

In answer to the Disciple's question in Matthew 18 as to who the greatest in the kingdom is, Jesus declared, *"the one who makes himself as little as this little child is the greatest in the kingdom of heaven"* (JB).

As children then, our responsibility revolves solely around loving God in return, and loving those he brings our way, by walking humbly in grace and faith. Re-aligning our values to God's rightside-up kingdom will allow us to live lives of greatness before God. The last *will* be first.

FOR GOD SO LOVED THE WORLD THAT HE EMBRACED US ALL. HE CROSSED THE OCEANS OF OUR SIN, ENTERED OUR SLAVERY, BROUGHT LIGHT INTO OUR DARKNESS, AND WALKED US TO THE FOOT OF HIS CROSS.

Being known by God is the criteria for being great in God's economy.

Hound of Heaven (excerpt)

Now of that long pursuit
Comes on at hand the bruit;
That Voice is round me like a bursting sea:

"And is thy earth so marred,
Shattered in shard on shard?
Lo, all things fly thee, for thou fliest Me!
Strange, piteous, futile thing,
Wherefore should any set thee love apart?
Seeing none but I makes much of naught"
(He said),
"And human love needs human meriting:
How hast thou merited
Of all man's clotted clay the dingiest clot?
Alack, thou knowest not
How little worthy of any love thou art!
Whom wilt thou find to love ignoble thee,
Save Me, save only Me?

All which I took from thee I did but take,
Not for thy harms,
But just that thou might'st seek it in My arms.
All which thy child's mistake
Fancies as lost, I have stored for thee at home:
Rise, clasp My hand, and come."

Halts by me that footfall:
Is my gloom, after all,
Shade of His hand, outstretched caressingly?

"Ah, fondest, blindest, weakest,
I am He Whom thou seekest!
Thou dravest love from thee, who dravest Me."

Francis Thompson

Chapter 9

Heaven's Heavyweight

Mixed Martial Arts – MMA – bothers me. I can admire the skill and athleticism necessary, but I just can't get thrilled with the idea of one person getting paid to pummel someone else into submission or render their opponent unconscious. It hits too close to real life. It's too gladiatorial to be classified as sport; politics, maybe, religion, definitely.

In the past, ashamedly, I was part of a church that functioned like an MMA ring, especially toward women. We've probably all seen it—seminary heavyweights, with control and authority over the pulpit or office. Hired shepherds who abuse the power differential in what ultimately descends into a spiritual bout of who has the bigger doctrinal muscles or legalistic leverage. Pugilistic priests and pastors: what a concept.

These men had trained hard. They knew how and where to look for weakness. Pow!—they'd hit you with a verse on the authority of elders from James. Smack!—upside the head with a quote concerning women in leadership from Paul. Zing!—with a stinger about submission from Jesus. And if someone remained standing, defiantly gentle, still seeking Scripture, they would assume a pained, comforting expression before lambasting your sorry-ass soul with some

Calvin or Luther, or something from Augustine or Aquinas, to illustrate their "God-given" right as keepers of truth. Can I get a witness?

I grew up in Africa and spent most of my professional life in the Middle East, where I researched and experienced the cultures, languages, and landscapes of the Bible, literally from the ground up. As a result, I began to read the biblical narratives through the eyes of a historical anthropologist, to understand plays on words, to appreciate just how counter-cultural Jesus actually is as he encounters the gamut of the populace. Whether engaging the top religious leaders or the lowest, leprous outcast, his compassion and kingdom-focus ring ever true. The stories come to life in vibrant, authentic, and sometimes raw ways. From religious authorities of his day to ours, little has changed. Hear his words anew. *"Whoever has ears to hear, whoever has eyes to see."*

On multiple occasions the religious authorities of Jesus' day went out of their way to pick fights with him, usually in an attempt to teach the young Galilean upstart proper temple etiquette, or how to obey rules about rules, or simply to exert their acquired authority over a young Rabbi who refused to be cowed by title or vestment. Usually Jesus shunned such squabbles, preferring to chat with tax collectors, the formerly demon-possessed, or prostitutes. Jesus knew full well who he was. That was enough for him.

On one rare occasion, however, a village slut, chancing

upon him, picked a fight, assessing him to be an easy target, a mere fly weight. She purposed to have a bit of fun. Jesus obliged her a quick bout. In fact, he had specifically gone out of his way, to a small Samaritan village called Sychar, just to conclude his divine appointment with this lady. It's quite dramatic actually. They meet at high noon, a fair distance from town.

Deliberately, she chooses this time of day in order to avoid any conversation. Before entering the physical space by the well, she pauses, scans the layout and seeing only a religiously observant Jew sitting there, guesses she will be spared any mindless chit chat. *He'll have nothing to do with me, and I sure want nothing to do with him, the self-righteous prig.*

Silently, Jesus watches this unfolding pantomime before opening innocently enough with a friendly "Shalom" and a request for a drink, a common courtesy in the Middle East. In this context, however, it was unexpected. A religious Jew would have had nothing to do with a Samaritan, or a woman, especially one with her reputation.

She stops, looks him over in earnest, and in essence states, "What's your game, chump? I know the rules far better than most. Are you really that stupid?"

Jesus smiles. He has piqued her interest. "If you truly knew the rules you would be asking me for pointers. I'm the Master." He indicates her water carrier. "I offer living water, not this stale stuff you've known all your life."

The woman licks her lips as she puts on her gloves, smirks, and begins to dance around the ring. "OK wise guy, let's go a few rounds since you think you're so special. You got no bucket." Right jab. "You got no rope." Left jab. "So how're you going to get any water out of this well, let alone fresh, clear, spring water?" A couple body blows with a quick right upper cut. "You think you're something?" Quick left again to take his eye off her up-coming right hook. "You greater than our Daddy Jacob who dug this well and gave it to us, us and our cattle?"

Jesus easily deflects her assault and smiles. He's got his fists up and is dancing around now, taking her punches. "Anyone who ever drank your well water got thirsty again, right?" Light jab. "That's not what I have to offer." Left feint. "You drink what I've got, you won't ever have to thirst again." He plants a soft right aside her head. "In fact, what I got becomes an artesian well, springing forth with such abundance that it eventually leads to eternal life." Quick left uppercut stopping just on the chin.

She steps back a bit dazed. *He really could have hurt me there.* "Yeah, right, Mr. Smarty-pants." She tries to land a hard right hook. It glances off. "If what you are saying is true, I would never again have to come out here in the heat of the day and talk to losers like you." Her left uppercut is shy.

Jesus draws back a step.

She follows in, thinking this an advantage.

"Go call your husband," Jesus says. Two quick, straight lefts stop a half-inch from her right eye, then a strong body-blow stops, resting a half inch from her *solar plexus*, an inch from her heart.

She blinks. The woman steps back again, reeling. *He could have pulverized me.* Anger infuses her and she lunges violently at Jesus. He sidesteps. She goes sprawling. She's bloodied and bruised. Skinned knees, ears ringing, eye is puffing up, lip is split and nose bright red.

Jesus gently picks her up and slowly shakes his head. Tears well in his eyes as he tries to dust her off.

She will have none of that. "I have no husband." The niceties are over. She swings wildly, frantic, hoping to land a lucky punch.

Jesus receives her aggression, deflecting her power. "Finally you give me a real answer." Light touch under her chin. "Number six has promised you everything, but so far has not delivered." A light bop atop her head.

Taking this again as a sign of weakness she renews her threats. "OK, I admit you got some talent, but I've just been messing with you," she mumbles through her gloves, now close to her face, and peeks through. "I know Mixed Martial Arts." She comes at him with a flying kick. "You bastards tore our temple down so now we have to worship atop a heap of ruins. And you got a new, fancy temple going up in Jerusalem. None of our early fathers ever worshiped there, but they did worship here." She attempts a back sweep with her legs. "You don't even know your history or what constitutes true religion." She comes in with fists swinging.

With one hand Jesus catches hold of both her fists, squares

his shoulders and slowly lets his arm drop to his side. He smiles. "Woman, dear, dear woman, true worship of the true Father takes place not atop stone ruins, or entombed inside them. But here." He taps his heart. "God is not a commodity to be bought and sold, or fought over. God is seeking true worshipers, those who know God is bigger than our beliefs and ideas of him. He earnestly seeks those who worship deeply in spirit and in truth." Jesus waits for a response.

Her hands are still up, but now she is looking over her gloves, not through them, wondering if this is some gimmick or a new form of dirty fighting. "Whatever, dude. All I know is that someday the Messiah will show up and kick your weaselly butt."

"Ta-dah." Jesus smiles and, with outstretched arms, merrily laughs. "He just did."

Her hands drop to her sides, defenseless. Her ashen face tells her whole life story. She turns and starts running.

"Lady, your water jar." Jesus calls after her.

She turns around, tears streaming down her radiant face. "That's far too small a container to hold living water, wouldn't you say? I need to go get the entire village. Wait for me?"

"Believe me, woman." He beams with joy. "You can count on it."

GOD IS NOT A COMMODITY TO BE BOUGHT AND SOLD, OR FOUGHT OVER. GOD IS SEEKING TRUE WORSHIPERS, THOSE WHO KNOW GOD IS BIGGER THAN OUR BELIEFS AND IDEAS OF HIM.

Essay on Man (excerpt)

Know then thyself, presume not God to scan;
The proper study of mankind is Man.
Placed on this isthmus of a middle state,
A being darkly wise and rudely great:
With too much knowledge for the Sceptic side,
With too much weakness for the Stoic's pride,
He hangs between; in doubt to act or rest,
In doubt to deem himself a God or Beast,
In doubt his mind or body to prefer;
Born but to die, and reasoning but to err;
Alike in ignorance, his reason such
Whether he thinks too little or too much:
Chaos of thought and passion, all confused;
Still by himself abused, or disabused;
Created half to rise and half to fall;
Great lord of all things, yet a prey to all;
Sole judge of truth, in endless error hurled:
The glory, jest, and riddle of the world!

Alexander Pope

Chapter 10

Know Thyself

I grew up a missionary kid. In fifth grade, believing I understood my faith, I would terrorize the "non-believers" during recess. If they did not convert to my understanding of Christianity, I, ashamedly, threatened to beat them up. I gained few friends and fewer converts. I shudder now at the childish conceit that imagined I had acquired God's edict to speak his mind for him.

Sole judge of truth, in endless error hurled:
The glory, jest, and riddle of the world!

Indeed!

Besides our loss of Eden, another foundational element has been lost to us by our sinning—light. Outside of God, there is no glory. In the full light of God's glory, our nakedness, our inability to add to God's redeeming work, *is* glory. Abandonment, therefore, to his full, grace-given sufficiency, despite our gross imperfections, illuminates his glory.

Back in the Garden of Eden, when Adam and Eve first viewed themselves as naked, they grew ashamed. Their physical condition had not changed, only their perception of self *vis-a-vis* God. What then enabled them to identify their nakedness? By rejecting God's provision, they put on shame.

Having divested themselves of innocence, they scrambled to mask their newly known immodesty. Within their fallen state, striving to provide their own covering, they grabbed for fig leaves. Now, clothing ourselves with any identity outside of who we truly are in God creates and then exacerbates this awareness of our inadequacy, our own newly discovered spiritual nakedness.

And we are naked. On all levels we are naked, especially spiritually. The shame of our nakedness, however, elicits embarrassment only as we reject God's provision and attempt to clothe ourselves, covering our spiritual indecency with cultures and totems, philosophies and ideologies, doctrines and traditions—anything that distinguishes us, divests us, vivisects us from our truer, childlike, God-intended humanity.

Allow me to illustrate. For five years, Diane and I ministered in what the Romans termed Arabia Felix, the "Blessed Yemen." A very conservative culture, men still dress like we imagine Abraham to have dressed, and women are fully veiled. Once, while driving to the Red Sea for our traditional Christmas-break camping trip, crossing a deserted area far from any habitation, I noticed up ahead a person walking on the road. Now, in Yemen, this was not uncommon. But this person happened to be stark naked. In Yemen, that *was*

uncommon.

When I slowed to see if there was a reason for such doings, it became clear by the pink plastic bag he wore as a hat, the axle grease he had smeared all over his body, and his very loud singing and erratic dancing that he was in fact insane. Wishing to minimize this spectacle in front of our preschoolers, I simply stated, "Well, that's not a sight you see every day." To which our four year old replied, "Yeah, because walking on the road is dangerous." Oh, to again view our shattered world through the innocent eyes of a child.

Similarly, we now dress ourselves up in wealth and power, progressivism and science, conservatism and conformity, all in an attempt to hide our spiritual nakedness and indecency. Yet we are not clothed by these, we simply are lacquered. Like that lunatic dancing on the road, we smear a rancid covering of pretended relevancy and self-importance over ourselves, and, *sans* clothing, go on parade.

In church now, we don funky hats or impressive vestments and sing or protest too loudly. We have crowned ourselves emperors of our insane little empires and, fully naked, despite claiming our sufficiency in Christ, we behave as if we might save ourselves. Even a simple child can see we are indecent. "Daddy, how come the Emperor has no clothes?" Could something be amiss?

The classical Greek word for glory connotes the aspects of brilliance and beauty; it is like the orange spot in our eyes, the afterglow, from looking at the sun. Where he reigns supreme, we, gloriously innocent-naked, solely clothed in God's grace, unashamed, bask in the divinity of our God-intended humanity *sans* the need to continually grasp for bigger and bigger fig leaves.

We now, however, stand surrounded by the multiple, fractured images of God's glory, which all religions proffer. None reflect even a poor icon or likeness of him. Like the story in 2013 that went viral on the internet of the 81 year old Spanish lady who, in attempting to honor an icon of Christ by "restoring it," added her measure of glory and inadvertently created an icon more akin to a monkey than one resembling Jesus, our attempts are all equally tragic. Her devotion and obvious passion notwithstanding, the outcome engendered outrage, ridicule, and some truly memorable memes and images on the web. Thankfully, a master was called in, the icon was re-restored, and one can again view the original intent.

Our own "monkey Jesus" renditions, no less comical but far more destructive, are imbued with our own culturally biased ideas, and temporal, historically founded identities as to what constitutes glory.

Equally, inversely, this complexity and madness which now comprise our fallen nature and frail human condition are integral, inbred components of sin's despoiling. Consequently, we have carefully crafted, politically minded, culturally focused, "Christianized" identities which throughout our history have produced warped justifications for crusades, inquisitions, colonialism, genocides of indigenous peoples, slavery, institutionalized injustice and racism, all baptized within a subtly perverse, salacious, autoerotic "God-be-for-us" mentality.

Jesus instructed his disciples,

"Beware of the scribes who like to walk about in long robes and love to be greeted obsequiously in the market squares, to take the front seats in the synagogues and the places of honor at banquets, who swallow the property of widows, while making a show of lengthy prayers. The more severe will be the sentence they receive."

Luke 20:46-47 NJB

Those who profit by such a cultural religion are hired shepherds who hide when calamity comes. God declares their condemnation is self-inscribed and severe.

Church history is replete with cultural Christianity's continual grabbing for bigger fig leaves. In the middle-ages, we purposely addicted God's poor to the opiate of absolution, demanding ecclesiastical authority as our due. Within our puritanical code in our "Manifest destiny," our claim to hate sin led to hating sinners and annihilating our "Canaanites." In more modern times, our drive to be a moral majority led us to dole out our own brand of loathing and condemnation, making ourselves not only irrelevant, but becoming sanctimonious jerks in the process.

And now, by claiming the edict to "subdue the Earth," we sanction the denuding of God's creation in the guise of "it's good for the economy." Believing we stand for justice, we perpetuate racism, xenophobia, and an underclass of working poor who simply "don't understand a good protestant work ethic." Jesus weeps.

We need continually to guard our hearts against the blatant refusal to embrace Christ's love and compassion for ourselves, our common humanity, and for his entire creation.

Whereas we are commissioned to invite all to the wedding feast of the God-groom and his bride, our actions and tenets too often slam shut the door to his church, safeguarding its "sanctity" from God's reckless love for the lost. How far removed this is from the lived-out, manifestly joyous gospel of Jesus. Such religious monkey business is blatant vandalism, defacing the true glory of God.

In every family and among our friends we have what we might call "our prodigals." Our compassion and hearts break for them because they are *our* "lost," our "sick," our "poor." But none are lost to God. He knows each of us. He loves and embraces each of us with everlasting arms, even if we have given up hope.

My niece, a beautiful and gifted young lady, finally, after many years of avoiding church due to spiritual traumas inflicted by a congregation more enamored with law than love, agreed to join us for a Sunday worship. Afterwards, an elderly lady walked up to her and stated, "I just have to tell you your tattoos offend me."

My niece blinked and gave an ashen-faced smile. She had trusted us. She had believed our heart and probably was aching to believe God's heart for her, too. But law came in, struck from the shadows, and injected its righteous venom. Religious propriety snatched away the little grace our niece had embraced, and the lady walked away happy in her self-righteousness, contented, having done God's work for him. And Jesus wept.

Daily, Churchianics steal away what little grace ekes out our church doors. Tattoos, an external symbol of identity, offend more than words issued from cancerous hearts of the self-righteous who hate God through hating people?

WHEREAS WE ARE COMMISSIONED TO INVITE ALL TO THE WEDDING FEAST OF THE GOD-GROOM AND HIS BRIDE, OUR ACTIONS AND TENETS TOO OFTEN SLAM SHUT THE DOOR TO HIS CHURCH, SAFEGUARDING ITS "SANCTITY" FROM GOD'S RECKLESS LOVE FOR THE LOST.

Such cultural Christianity, the antithesis of a Christ-centered, loving relationship, can become a form of religionism barely indistinguishable from other faiths whose spiritual founders have not called upon their disciples to love their enemies and pray for those who persecute them.

My niece's story does not end there. Just as he did on the cross, Jesus' grace steals in to overcome law, overpower hate, and remove sin's stain. Whereas the law kills, grace embraces. The Spirit offers freedom and life. Choosing grace, enfolded now in Christ's healing, we together continue to seek to live in joy rather than condemnation. Through her vibrant art, she extends hope and grace by painting the humanity and beauty of those who are homeless.

Having ministered among Muslims, we have seen people embrace the Gospel, many out of what we considered impossible circumstances. I am reminded of one young fanatical religious leader who carried a fatwa, or religious edict, giving him permission to arrest or execute Christians in the city of Damascus in Syria. One could even call him a terrorist. Just outside of the city, however, he had a vision of Christ.

This young convert became an advocate of the faith, and eventually even a missionary, writing many books of Christian apologetics. Here was a religious radical bent on harming Christians, and Jesus reached down and saved him instead of calling in a drone strike for a clean kill.

In the months following 9/11, I shared this narrative with our sending church and supporters challenging them that if Christ could save this man, should we not also be praying that God would reveal himself to Osama Bin Laden in the same saving way?

In response, we received some nasty, disturbing e-mails, some even from our church leadership. We were accused, among other things, of being anti-American and having "gone native." I was baffled.

Some had apparently missed the patently obvious, that the original story had taken place nearly two thousand years previous and the young man, named Saul, came from a town in Turkey, called Tarsus. Only later had he changed his name to Paul. He preferred, however, to call himself the "chief of sinners."

Given the political sentiments, Christ's command to love our enemies and pray for those who persecuted us had evidently become an inconvenient truth.

Setting ourselves and our culture as the standard rather than the radical Kingdom Jesus brings, inevitably reduces God to an idea, a knowledge-set, a litany of do's and don'ts. Thus we render a "monkey Jesus" religion. No longer comical, it is rightly ridiculed and fully deserving of outrage and derision.

Right relationship is the trusting child, content in her Father's embrace. Religious monkey business is spiritual terrorism.

Christ's freely offered forgiveness can too easily be sold in exchange for penance and duty. In the Garden we expressed our dissatisfaction with God's provision by demanding "more." Our original sin was not merely pride, it was an unmitigated thirst for more than God's full sufficiency, his provision of all things good. We wanted knowledge of both good and evil. God's standard remains too high. He calls us to be perfect even as he is perfect. Our naked state screams this an impossible calling, and thus we lower the bar. We forge answers for our fears, excuses for our inadequacies. We have everything in Christ, and yet we still seek to add our own measure to God's sufficiency. In essence we add guilt to grace, fear to love, junk to Jesus.

As C. S. Lewis reminds us, "It would seem that Our Lord finds our desires not too strong, but too weak. We are half-hearted creatures . . . when infinite joy is offered us, like an ignorant child who wants to go on making mud pies in a slum because he cannot imagine what is meant by the offer of a holiday at sea. We are far too easily pleased."

SETTING OURSELVES AND OUR CULTURE AS THE STANDARD RATHER THAN THE RADICAL KINGDOM JESUS BRINGS, INEVITABLY REDUCES GOD TO AN IDEA, A KNOWLEDGE-SET, A LITANY OF DO'S AND DON'TS.

Heaven has no room for my measure of being. Heaven is complete as it is. I can bring nothing into heaven without making it less complete. Therefore, when my mortal flesh dies, what is sown remains corruptible, weak, temporal. In I Corinthians 15 St. Paul alludes to our bodies as seeds.

We smile at a child who imagines that by planting an acorn, a "gianter" acorn would grow, for we know differently. At the resurrection, what is raised up is something new, a thing beyond measure. Our spirits then, embody a radically other type of God-intended creation. A new, spiritually fitted 'body' awaits us, as unlike our present one as the acorn is from the oak. The acorn lasts a season. The oak lives on, growing, flourishing, offering shade and shelter for centuries.

When this mortal seed therefore—corrupted, disabled,

naked and alone—dies, if I have indeed nurtured and cultivated the truer spiritual seed-kernel of that being within me—that God-bestowed relational strand of DNA from our Creator's original design—what germinates, thankfully, humbly, miraculously, becomes a majestic, oak-like creation fit for so much more than Eden.

Rom. 5:15-16; 19 JB

"Adam prefigured the One to come, but the gift itself considerably outweighed the fall. If it is certain that through one man's fall so many died, it is even more certain that divine grace, coming through the One man, Jesus Christ, came to so many as an abundant free gift. The results of the gift also outweigh the results of one man's sin: for after one single fall came judgment with a verdict of condemnation, now after many falls comes grace with its verdict of acquittal. – As by one man's disobedience (the) many were made sinners, so by One man's obedience (the) many will be made righteous."

Chapter 11

Madam, I'm Adam

A raspy cough grips his chest again and, with dagger-long nails, squeezes. Adam is dying, he knows, and grateful, finally, for the prospect. Perhaps Sheol contains rest, perhaps not. It no longer matters. What else could God bring to him, or rather take away, in the grave? In a way, he views his thousands of years of suffering, this, his living grief, as a retort to those who want God only to be good. Adam, the original sinner, accepts this role. He despises it as well.

Passover once again threatens to pass without a true Paschal lamb. Since his exile from Eden, loneliness has methodically etched Adam's years with its iron stylus, leaving deep, haunting scars in his leather-hard heart. None of his great, great, great, etc. grandchildren remember him. A thousand million of his offspring, nameless, along with Eve, his wife, now lay locked in their graves. *Alone*. Perhaps faith serves merely as an excuse for not dying. Perhaps hope simply is another word for make-believe.

Adam shuffles his wearied, frail frame through the crowded Jerusalem streets, all the while being jostled and battered by the throng earnest for the Passover day of preparation. Adam pushes against the mob, to survive the press, to prove that he still matters.

Exhaustion and his aloneness, however, finally master him. He hunkers down amidst the morning's refuse, protected by a series of the cardo pillars, and rests. At his foot, maggots pulse through some rotten scrap of food. Flies buzz affectionately.

Without permission, tears begin to roll silently down his weathered, sallow cheeks. Futility gathers around him like his tattered cloak, a deep sigh wracking his frame. He cups his head in his hands and quietly rocks back and forth on his heels and begins, for the hundred-millionth time, to pray through his tears, "My God, my God, why have you deserted me? How far from saving me, these words I groan!" He gazes at the maggots at play. His tears run hot . . . "Yet here I am, now more a worm than a man." There is not even an echo from the bronzed heavens. Adam utterly is without Eden.

Suddenly, angry shouting grows, ringing down the street from where he sits cloistered. He shudders at its familiarity: the incessant drum, the crass, vulgar laughter, this parade initiated by screeching street urchins. It all adds up to another processional: a winding, writhing, serpent of those condemned to a tortured death.

Adam's last ember of hope wanes. *Even at Passover they crucify my children.* He shuffles. Slinking further back against the wall by his pillar, he slouches, unevenly bent. Deepening darkness shrouds his world. This scene has played itself out hundreds of times in Jerusalem since that new procurator, Pilate, arrived.

His heart grows sick as the first man passes, the face, diabolical, marred by dirt and blood. A wooden plank swings from his neck, the convict's name and crime clearly printed in Hebrew, Latin and Greek – "Cain - Murderer - Rebel."

A second man passes, his face obscured by bloodied ropes of matted hair. His back torn open, flies feasting. Tied to his heavy cross beam, he grimaces with each step. His feet, beaten with clubs. His placard reads – "Abel - Malcontent - Self-righteous."

Then a new sound is heard. Something eerily different. Adam straightens up to take in the oddity. Weeping, wailing, women screaming in pain and outrage. *This is new! Women at a crucifixion?* Normally the screaming comes from the convicts or the curses from the crowd. But this crying carries sorrow, pregnant with anguish's heavy, demanding burden.

A third criminal, beaten and bloodied, lurches forward in faltering steps. His hair dripping a vile crimson. A yarmulke of thorns, a crown of derision, sits affixed to his scalp. His beard is patchy where clumps have been pulled out. Rich stains leak through his robe, a sign of having been scourged. The board states his name and crime, "Second Adam – Traitor to the Crown – King of a Subjected People."

Adam's eyes grow wide. Fear, bewilderment, outrage. No word can describe the void, the heaviness, the growing awareness of his loss of comprehensibility. Adam does not know if his voice gives utterance as the condemned man stumbles, crashing face first onto the pavement with a sickening, jarring, crunching thud.

For the first time, recognizing up close what he had only seen from afar, Adam sees Jesus face-to-face. Eyes meet.

The question. The answer. The empty life of not knowing. The banishment. The silence of God echoing down the corridors of his life. The barred gates to Eden. God's tears. The searching. The prayers that bounced down upon his head from the bronzed heavens. All these Adam lives again in a single heartbeat.

What can he do but follow.

The place of the skull had been a shallow quarry left from the construction of the northern gate. The central outcropping, comprised of poor quality limestone, had subsequently been abandoned. Upon this stone, the stone the builders rejected, the crucified are hung to die. The main road north passes adjacent to it. Rome understands a geo-political feature when she sees one.

By the time Adam has limped out of the gate and up the main road a pace, three crosses have been elevated, silhouetted against a blanched, sullen morning sky. Adam stares at Jesus as minutes fade into hours, watching as his breathing becomes more strained. "Why have so many had to die?" he asks eventually, matter-of-factly.

Through a grimaced smile, Jesus answers. "There is but one death, Adam. But in me shall all be made alive. Now is come to pass the saying, 'Oh Grave, where is your sting? Oh Death, where is your victory?' This Temple they will destroy. In three days, I will raise it up."

For three sharp, hard hours darkness persists. Jesus hangs motionless, breathing a slow, rasping rhythm. Superstitious soldiers keep their distance, talking in hushed tones. The raging religious authorities gloat. Then just as suddenly, the darkness fades. People agitate again.

Jesus straightens himself as best he can, pushing against the nails in his feet. Taking a deep breath, and to everyone's amazement, he starts triumphantly to sing Psalm twenty-two. "Eli, Eli, lama sabachthani?"

Adam, in wonder, stands. Amidst the confusion, he remembers singing the same Psalm, earlier that very morning, while he lay amidst the fallenness of this world. "My God, my God, why have you forsaken me?" And now, Jesus has taken up the Psalm, nailed to a cross.

Adam sings, reciting the rest of the lyric in his head. He has gotten to the lines, "My strength is trickling away, my bones are all disjointed," when Jesus cries aloud, "It . . . is . . . Fulfilled!"

Immediately, the earth begins to undulate, progressively growing to a swaying that causes Adam to lose his balance. By the time the earth has stopped quaking, Jesus is dead.

Adam stands in awe. Jesus had sung the entire Psalm, even to the last line. Adam quotes aloud, "And those who are dead, their descendants will serve him, will proclaim his name to generations still to come; and these will tell of his saving justice to a people yet unborn: it is fulfilled." Adam, noticing the ashen faces of the religious authorities, knows they too have not missed the implications of what has just happened. They have crucified the King of Glory.

Adam again looks at Jesus' lifeless body, contorted, caked in darkened blood. Then he sees her, Mary, Jesus' mother, sobbing quietly at the cross base. She recognizes Adam. He acknowledges her. She nods. He humbly, reverently bows.

So this is HIS answer.

Adam has yet to taste death. He is still on his Jesus field trips. Occasionally, he can be seen wandering the empty streets of a ravaged war zone, rummaging amidst the ruins of an earthquake, stopping at each door in the pediatric oncology ward of a university hospital.

That horrific image of Jesus on his cross still haunts Adam's dreams and gnaws at his wakefulness; the Second Adam up there, life slipping away heartbeat by heartbeat, not even enough breath to utter the sorrow, the pain, the compassion that sculpted Christ's face. And then the odd serenity that suffused it all.

But also there was Abel. Abel, his son, found, forgiven, free. Jesus, with crooked smile, declaring, "Today, will you be with me. We're going Home."

Adam sighs.

Daily Adam sees it, Jesus' eternally efficacious blood dripping from that limp, battered body, congealing, forming little carnelian stalactites from the elbows, the chin, the nail-bound feet of the incarnated flesh of the Eternal King of Glory.

And then silence.

All sufficient.

Paid in full.

Whereas the Angels shook heaven with the announcement

of his birth, at his death, they could only stand in wonder, silent and in awe. When Jesus rose again, the only sounds were the breaking of Hell's Gates, and Hell's chains that bound us to fear and death, accompanied by the shriek of the enemy being crushed under foot by him who has risen indeed.

Each Easter now we declare it—"He is risen, Christ is risen indeed."

That is the gospel, the good news. What was once dead has been made alive. What was once broken and maimed is now made whole. What was cursed is now the ultimate blessing. The cross truly is victory. In truth, Christ is risen.

What is so stark in this statement is that Jesus answers Pilate's, and ultimately our question—"What is truth?"

No longer is an answer wanting. In fact, by Christ rising from the dead, he answers that question, and any other question there might have been. Is there life after death? "He is risen!" Does God exist? "He is risen." What about the problem of evil? "He is risen."

THAT IS THE GOSPEL, THE GOOD NEWS. WHAT WAS ONCE DEAD HAS BEEN MADE ALIVE. WHAT WAS ONCE BROKEN AND MAIMED IS NOW MADE WHOLE. WHAT WAS CURSED IS NOW THE ULTIMATE BLESSING. THE CROSS TRULY IS VICTORY. IN TRUTH, CHRIST IS RISEN.

Every fear is quelled, every hunger satisfied. There can only be joy and hope where once there was deep, abiding fear and doubt. Like Adam, like Job, like Spafford, we need not have all the answers. In faith we apprehend the only one that matters: he is risen. In all truth, he is risen indeed.

Read again that Romans passage at the chapter heading.

Christ's freely given, efficacious death and resurrection so far outweigh the original sin and fall of one man, that by God's divine grace, where once we lived condemned, we now live acquitted and righteous. This God did. Jesus paid it all.

The only thing left to bring to what God already has accomplished is a child-like faith within an open heart.

Even as exiles out of Eden, amidst that long, deathly silence of God, whirling in mystery, he whispers to us his good news. We need only be still and know he is God. Journeying with us on our Jesus field trips, he bestows enough hope, sufficient grace, his abiding peace, and an added measure of faith for us to quietly, gratefully weep forth our eternal hallelujah.

CHRIST'S FREELY GIVEN, EFFICACIOUS DEATH AND RESURRECTION
SO FAR OUTWEIGHS THE ORIGINAL SIN AND FALL OF ONE MAN,
THAT BY GOD'S DIVINE GRACE, WHERE ONCE WE LIVED CONDEMNED,
WE NOW LIVE ACQUITTED AND RIGHTEOUS. THIS GOD DID.
JESUS PAID IT ALL.

Dabbling

Ankle-deep in the Sea that is God
I kick the foam of receding waves.
Careful not to get too wet,
I dabble and splash as a child.

Fearful to swim too deep and sink,
I venture offshore with a lifeline
That holds me safe to temporal things
Lest tides of devotion wash me out to sea.

What matters in life is that step beyond;
Out of our depth, out of self-control.
If I have not swum in the Sea that is God
It matters nothing what I have done instead.

Samuel C. Walker

About the Author

Privileged to be born and raised in East Africa by missionary parents, Sam, with his own family, subsequently spent over fifteen years living, teaching, and ministering in the Middle East (Yemen, Israel/West Bank, Jordan), engaged in projects as varied as archaeology, sustainability, reconciliation, teaching and writing. He is a professor of historical geography of the Bible, anthropology, ancient history and comparative religions. For seven years he worked in Micronesia researching and addressing climate-change issues related to food, water and energy security.

In July of 2014 he and his family returned from research in the UNESCO World Heritage Site of Aksum, Ethiopia, where he set up projects for archaeology and taught at the Aksum University. He holds an MA from the University of Leicester, England in archaeology and heritage studies, both a BS & MS from Western Oregon University in interdisciplinary studies (history & sciences) and education, and a BA from Westmont College, Santa Barbara, CA in comparative religions. Sam is a published author in areas of archaeology, sustainability, and reconciliation, has taught in universities internationally and in the US, and has presented at many conferences in the areas of missions, leadership training, pastoral care, sustainability, and archaeology/heritage.

Sam currently splits his time between Seattle, Washington and Ethiopia. His wife, Diane and four of their five children, Chris, Hilary, Byron and Colin, with much hope and love, anticipate being reunited soon with their adopted daughter, Letebrhan, from Ethiopia.

Publisher

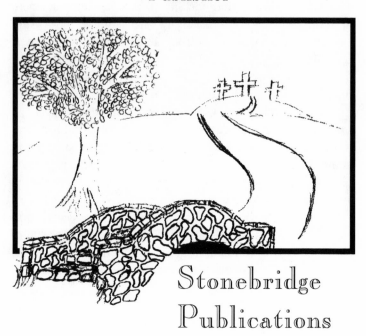

Stonebridge

Publications

FOR MORE GREAT TITLES, VISIT STONEBRIDGEPUBLICATIONS.COM